ARTS AND CRAFTS OF
INDIA

NICHOLAS BARNARD

Photographs by
ROBYN BEECHE

CONRAN OCTOPUS

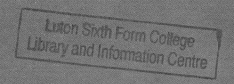
00035041
745.0954

First published in 1993 by
Conran Octopus Limited
37 Shelton Street
London WC2H 9HN

This paper back edition published in 1995
by Conran Octopus Limited

Reprinted 1996

Art editor: **Karen Bowen**
In-house editor: **Denny Hemming**
Copy editor: **Ralph Hancock**
Editorial assistant: **Jane Chapman**
Production: **Mano Mylvaganam**

Consultant to Conran Octopus:
Dr Asok K. Das,
Senior Visiting Research Fellow,
Victoria & Albert Museum, London

Map: **Line + Line**

British Libary Cataloguing-in-Publication Data
A catalogue record for this book is available from
the British Library

ISBN 1 85029 705 3

Typeset by **Avocet Typesetters**, Bicester, Oxon
Printed and bound in Singapore

THE CARVER OF STONE

Every Hindu pilgrim centre across India is host to a wealth of craftsmen who create all manner of household deities for the family shrine. Bathed by the early morning winter sunlight, this soapstone carver awaits his custom near the entrance to the temple complex at Nathdwara in Rajasthan (page 1).

THE PAINTER OF CLOTH

Looking on in adoration, these gopis (milkmaids) are the loving consorts of the ever playful and endearingly popular god Krishna, to whom this temple hanging, or pichvai, from Rajasthan is dedicated (pages 2/3).

THE EMBROIDERESS

Sprinkled across the scrublands of Kutch in the western state of Gujarat are communities and encampments of pastoralists who are dedicated to the art and craft of embroidery. An essential requisite for the dowry, embroideries such as this odhni (headshawl) will be worked with loving devotion by the mother of the bride (page 5).

CONTENTS

FOREWORD

Work is worship

ROADSIDE BILLBOARD, THAR DESERT, RAJASTHAN

What an extraordinary experience it is to visit India for the first time! From the moment of arrival, one cannot fail to be bewildered, a little frightened, and mostly lost in awe at the pressing immediacy of energy and work. Whatever the task, be it trivial or extraordinary, all around men and women are labouring, and the air crackles with the exuberance of Indian life.

In the old quarters of the towns and cities, down narrow back streets, communities of craftsmen continue to fulfil the demands of rich and poor alike, while beyond the frenetic city street scenes, far from the historic monuments and industrial estates, the peoples of India continue to live and work to patterns little changed over the millennia. Outside the urban centres, the vast majority — some eighty-five per cent of a population of nearly 900 million — are bound to the life of the village and countryside, subject to the fickle rhythms of the monsoon.

No matter how fleeting a visit to this exotic country may be, it is impossible not to gain an inkling of the creative genius and overwhelming fecundity of the arts and crafts of both urban and village communities. By the side of a busy city road weavers can be seen at work preparing the cotton or silk thread which will later be mounted on their wooden looms. In the city jewellery bazaar the silversmith can be found, bent with intense concentration over his intricate filigree work. On the open road potters and their wives are a common sight, swaying under the weight of a carbuncled cluster of voluminous clay water pots, borne on their heads as they walk from their village to the market.

This book is an introduction to the life and work of the craftsmen and women of today's India. So widespread and diverse are the country's arts and crafts that a comprehensive survey of the history and continuing vitality of such creativity would demand the work of at least a decade and would fill, with image and word, a score of volumes. Instead, this work attempts to serve as a colourful preface to the topic, an appetizer akin to the delicious north Indian roadside snack known as *chaat*, rather than as a grandiose state banquet or wedding feast. The aim is to awaken the senses and stimulate the appetite for the experiences that follow.

And indeed, the creation of this book is the result of an odyssey, marked by a succession of happy events that we shall always savour. Ever seeking the craftspeople of India, we have followed the visual, audible and olfactory clues of the land, coming intimately to know such creative sounds as the clack of the heddles and the spooling of the shuttle at the loom, the clink of hammers and chisels on metal. The sight of balconies and rooftops overflowing with the bright colour and lively patterning of thousands of cotton headshawls drying in the bright sun never fails to excite the eye; and often, halting on the fringe of a village, the nose twitches with pleasure at the scent of that particular fragrance of wood and straw smoke that comes from the firing of an open kiln, packed like a lumpy mattress with a cache of elegant terracotta pots.

Not only have we been stimulated and delighted by the discovery and recording of the work of craftsmen and women within village, town and city, but we have also been welcomed with open-hearted generosity and spirited hospitality. This quality of friendship, combined with a patient and often bemused indulgence of our needs, enabled us to complete our work with pleasure. To these craftsmen and women, and to our friends, companions and guides in India whether newly met or known over the years, we respectfully dedicate this book.

In the south of India the harvest festival of Pongal is joyfully commemorated by the daily act of decorating the threshold of the home with auspicious symbols. This kolam depicts a five-pointed star, a potent charm to ward off evil.

FOUNDATIONS AND INSPIRATIONS

As one journeys around the states and regions of India it is all too apparent that, despite the boundaries established by an independent nation, this is a land marked and divided by dramatic contrasts in terrain, history, culture and religious beliefs. To the west, the desert landscapes of Rajasthan and Gujarat are home to itinerant shepherds and proud farmers as well as the progeny of their once divine rulers. In the north, the Himalayan mountain range, thought to be the abode of the gods, feeds the waters of the sacred Ganges, which runs to the sea along an immense alluvial plain densely peopled by Hindu and Muslim alike. The eastern lands that line the route of the Ganges are also thronged with busy villages. All around, states such as Manipur, Nagaland and Assam, as well as the deep interior of Orissa and south-eastern Madhya Pradesh, are populated largely by the earlier inhabitants of India, known officially as 'tribals', whose arts and crafts are wholly alien to the later Aryan-dominated culture. Beyond Madhya Pradesh and Maharashtra, the south begins: amid rice paddies, thriving temple towns and hillside tea and spice farms the fine-boned and courteous Dravidian peoples are devoted to the maintenance of their independent culture and language.

THE WEST

If you turn left before the clock tower and walk through the old streets of Jodhpur town in the princely state of Rajasthan, dodging cycles, motor rickshaws and bold cows, you will eventually reach, after a dogleg to the right, the famous Muslim dyers' quarter. Go on any morning of the year, save Fridays or a rare day of rain, remembering that in order to keep one's bearings it is as well to look up now and then from within the cool shaded alleys of the bazaar to enjoy the sight of the splendid hill fort of the erstwhile ruling Rajput family, rising as a romantic backdrop to the rooftop collections of colourful tie-dyed cloth. By following the gutters, which run with a murky mixture of dyes, one arrives at the central square of the quarter, lined with the houses of the tie-dyeing community. From balcony and window to the dark recesses of the workshops, this *mohalla* or dwelling quarter is alive with the energy of the dyers' work. Whether they are tying cotton cloth into sections to exclude the dye, or dunking rolls of turbans in vats of colour, their stained hands, shirts and skirts declare them members of the *chippa* caste of dyers.

The work of these Rajasthani craftsmen and their fellow *rangrez* dyers is famed throughout western and northern India. Working in families or sharing commissions among a larger group, they fulfil the orders of intermediaries, merchants, shopkeepers and travelling salesmen, satisfying the insatiable demand of the village men and women of the region for brightly coloured and patterned turbans, scarves and shawls. Rajasthan lies at the heart of the 'colour belt' of India, an area that runs from the Indus basin to the Gangetic plains. The dyeing guilds and communities of the towns have provided, generation after generation, the vivid garments beloved by the people of these desert and scrub lands. So adaptable and robust is this craft that it is no wonder that the alien demands of the European, American and Japanese textile designers of the last decade have been easily met. This incongruous export production is often seen hanging out to dry amid the ranks of turmeric-bright village fashions, such as the *odhnis* or headshawls of the farmers' wives.

Leaving the intimacy of the old town and its narrow alleys full of the noise of a multitude of craftsmen, take a car or motor rickshaw up to the calm of the ramparts of Jodhpur fort. From here one may muse in relative isolation over the seeming emptiness and sterility of the Thar desert extending to each horizon, a rocky landscape dotted with thorn bushes and garnished with the ephemeral richness of a few irrigated fields. And yet it is in this arid region, once dense with forest and teeming with wildlife,

that the earliest remnants of man's creative presence in India have been found. Here, more than two and a half thousand years before the birth of Christ and a thousand years before the arrival of the Aryan nomads and their Hindu religion, there existed a spectacular urban culture.

Centred on the two major cities of Mohenjo Daro and Harappa, the Indus Valley civilization stretched over what is now the province of Sind in Pakistan through northern Rajasthan and the region known as Kathiawar in Gujarat, as well as the northern lands of the Punjab and Haryana. From archaeological finds it is obvious that a craft culture of some sophistication was well established by this time, serving the needs of both the local farming community and trade networks beyond the region. Indeed, it seems that an agrarian village culture developed throughout the subcontinent from this centre, formulating farming practices little altered today, and giving a ceaseless rhythm to the lives of an ever increasing population. It is also clear from the remains of this civilization that the crafts of India have been sought from far and wide across the trading world from a very early date. By the first century BC India was as

Much of Rajasthan is a harsh desert land dotted with communities of noble peoples proud of their warrior ancestry. Against a backdrop of dun landscapes, the exuberant display of brightly dyed and patterned textiles shows a heartfelt love of colour. Whether engaged in the daily chore of foraging for firewood (left) or tending the extended family of elders and children (above), the village women of Rajasthan are renowned for their colourful attire. Such a delight in colour extends to home decoration, as seen in historic towns such as Jodhpur (opposite) where streets are painted in vivid tones.

The traditional labours of the craftsmen of Rajasthan and Gujarat are seen on a grand scale at the many great religious and livestock festivals that are held at places of pilgrimage all over the region. Of these the Pushkar and Nagaur camel, cattle and buffalo fairs of Rajasthan have become well known. Undeterred by international curiosity the myriad clans, castes and tribes continue to congregate in large numbers, dressed in the finest dowry embroideries, block-printed garments and jewellery, which together establish their place and role in a rural society. At these festivals caste members from the district and region meet, contract and celebrate marriages, and perform religious rites.

It is also an appropriate occasion for the selling of a great range of local crafts as well as more exotic items from other states. Amid this throng of traders' stalls, the bards of the community recite and musicians play, while around them the camels, horses, donkeys and oxen are traded and races are run. The animals are not neglected at this time, and herdsmen are sorely tempted to purchase brightly coloured saddles, ropes and bridles (opposite below). Many a beast of burden is decorated with a lively array of auspicious designs, such as the clipped camel (opposite above) or the paint-daubed oxen, and others are lovingly caparisoned with colourful embroidered trappings on their backs, necks, ears, legs, chests, muzzles and horns.

Across the lands of Kutch in the state of Gujarat, amidst the salt pans, thorn-tree dotted scrub and rocky hillocks, live a variety of pastoralists who share a love of embroidery and lavish silver jewellery. Of these groups, the Rabari are well known as shepherds and camel owners. Following the pasture that carpets the scrublands after the monsoon, the camel trains are led by the women bearing water vessels on their heads (above), eased by a cloth-covered ondoni, or pot cushion. In the local market towns the men display their finest attire (right) and many of the younger women (opposite) continue to follow the convention of purdah.

open to international trade as it is today. And of this commerce the most enduring and successful example has been the production of bright-coloured, fast-dyed and patterned textiles, a craft that has attracted gold from the treasuries of successive civilizations and colonial empires. Today the descendants of these early craftsmen continue to flourish in the practice of their traditional skills throughout the western states of India, and nowhere more than in Rajasthan and Gujarat.

As a predominantly desert land of seasonal beauty and great contrasts in landscape, architecture and the garb of its people, Rajasthan draws many visitors. The forts, mansions, palaces and temples that dot the skyline in every quarter of the state are a testament to the wealth and the bellicose temperament of the ruling Rajput élite. Established as the rulers of warrior kingdoms from the seventh century AD, the Rajputs have resolutely resisted any attempts at subjugation, whether by Afghan, Mughal, Maratha or British empires. After more than a thousand years of their valiant deeds, it is no wonder that a thriving popular culture now exists, colourfully manifested in puppetry and theatre; in the murals of the painted houses, from mansions to mud huts; and in the exotically coloured clothing of the people, from their handsome turbans through hand-printed or tie-dyed shawls to vividly patterned, embroidered shoes.

To the south of Rajasthan lies the less visited yet wealthy state of Gujarat, characterized not only by a dynamically expanding industrial infrastructure, epitomized by the frenetic city of Ahmedabad, but also by its well organized and successful farming community centred on the districts of Saurashtra. In the far west, the sparsely peopled lands of Kutch and the adjacent salt pans are home to the self-contained enclaves of semi-nomadic pastoralists such as the Rabari, who shunned the temptations of modern life until very recently. The women are expert embroiderers, taking great delight in black attire made all the more striking by ornaments of red and silver needlework on blouse and skirt, and jangling swags of bright silver jewellery. For the younger women this finery is often partly concealed by a woollen tie-dyed headshawl of deepest jet, dotted with red or orange, which is worn throughout the year, despite the incapacitating heat of the summer months. On the open road it is always a thrilling sight to meet one of these footloose families with their baggage camels, and to watch with astonishment the accuracy with which the tall white-turbaned and -attired shepherds control their goats and sheep with a low cry, a gesture or, seemingly, by the power of thought.

Like Rajasthan, Gujarat possesses a thriving race of craftspeople, who have been well served by a network of trading ports whose names have entered the lore of early international

trade. Commerce with the Roman Empire was particularly successful, fed by the ports on the Gulf of Cambay and carried principally by Arab seafarers who had learnt to exploit the monsoon winds for their annual cycle of voyages. Indeed, it was these merchants who first carried the Islamic faith to India, and brought to the textile artisans of coastal Gujarat cosmopolitan influences from across the globe. As a precious cargo of Arab sailing dhows over the centuries, the exquisitely woven, printed or tie-dyed cloth was created to meet the demands of customers hailing from lands as distant as East and North Africa and the Indonesian archipelago.

Although many of the craft practices that once created the finest artefacts have been in decline for centuries, there is every evidence that the craftspeople of Gujarat are now thriving. Cushioned by their pedigree of creative ingenuity and enduring traditions, the weavers, embroiderers and dyers continue to meet the needs of the indigenous marketplace. Through the efforts of government agencies as well as philanthropic visitors, access has been established to a lively export market and appreciation for the work of India's master craftsmen is apparent from Japan to Germany.

THE NORTH

In a remote village clinging to the side of a desiccated mountain in the Zanskar range of Ladakh, an elderly silversmith sits cross-legged before his work. By his side a silver and copper prayer wheel awaits the final burnish that will give an added sparkle to the evocations of the new owner. Spread before him are the components of a famed Ladakhi teapot, wrought in copper and silver to a design that characterizes the extraordinary cultural mix of the region. He looks up as we approach and his weather-lined face, full of Central Asian character, creases into a welcoming smile, and we are motioned to sit close by the welcome warmth of his brazier.

The view from the workshop is one of stimulating beauty, forming an ethereal composition of castellated dun and tan mountain peaks cut out against a lapis sky, offset by the meandering line of immaculately tended riverine crops below. On the other side of the valley stands a monastery decked with brightly painted prayer wheels and flags that flutter in the wind, willing the pilgrims on as they climb the mountain paths to its sanctuary. Silenced by this scene, we neglect our host; and yet this is of no consequence, for the silversmith works on in peace, relishing the meditative atmosphere of this mountain preserve of the Buddhist faith.

After the sweltering bustle and noise of the Gangetic plains the ascent to the peace of the Ladakh mountain kingdom in the summer months provides one of the most striking contrasts for which northern India is renowned. From the Himalayan hill stations to the high Vale of Kashmir, the mountains to the north and north-west of the subcontinent have provided not only an opposite in climate and topography, but have also physically shielded the faiths and the cultures of the people of the plains. From time to time even that bulwark has been breached; yet the resultant confrontations and the ebb and flow of immigrants and invaders have instituted a series of complex cultural interchanges that have accommodated a multitude of faiths, and have brought inspiration to many a craftsman.

The first of these foreigners arrived around 1500 BC. These were the nomadic hordes who had originally emerged from the region of the Caspian Sea and the southern Russian steppes, and who spread far and wide in search of pasture, eventually settling in Greece, Asia Minor and Persia as well as India. Through the mountain passes these cattle-breeding and horse-riding people arrived, speaking a tongue belonging to the Indo-Aryan language group from which both Latin and Sanskrit are derived. These

Aryans knew little of the sophistication of the established Indian village life. Their religion and social order, however, were to change the face of Indian civilization. The Hindu religion, as collected in the 1028 hymns of the Rig Veda, is based on the tales, myths and legends of the Aryans; and their social order gave birth to the caste system. In return the sedentary villagers of the Indus region and beyond shared by intermarriage their knowledge of agriculture and craft, creating the social, economic and cultural foundations of the rural India of today.

For the next thousand years the Aryan culture spread southwards across India, and the specialist occupations of the community developed within it. The village craftsman served both the nomads and the settled farmers; the carpenter, as maker of the chariot and the plough, was foremost among his peers who included the metalworkers, potters, weavers and the basket and mat makers. Thriving groups of craftsmen began to trade beyond the immediate neighbourhood. To ease the carriage of raw materials and the distribution of finished goods, artisans tended to congregate, forming centres of industry which often, when strategically well placed, became towns. In these towns the communities were organized into *shreni* (guilds), each inhabiting a particular district and tending to become identified as a particular sub-caste in its own right.

*Life in Ladakh is in dramatic
contrast to that in the plains far
below the Himalayas. From the
monastery at Shey (above left)
the peace of the land is evident.
Buddhist culture permeates all
aspects of life, illustrated by the
prayer-wheel spinning silversmith
(right) and festival costumes
(above).*

In the midst of this Aryan colonization northern India witnessed the birth of another world religion. Seeking liberation from the world's suffering and the cycles of rebirth of the Hindu doctrine, the northern Indian prince Gautama Buddha and his followers established the Buddhist faith some 500 years before the birth of Christ. Embraced by the once bellicose Emperor Ashoka (268–231 BC) and disseminated within the splendid Mauryan empire, the creed united almost the whole of the subcontinent. This was a golden era of Buddhist-dominated learning, social organization and patronage of the arts and crafts, elevating select craftsmen to the employ of the court and so creating an important precedent. Lured by the prospect of rich booty, Alexander the Great ventured into northern India for two years from 327 BC, and although his territorial gains were limited to the far north-west they established a short-lived Greek colonial trading empire that stretched from the Mediterranean to the Indus Valley. More influential, however, were the creative exchanges

of this era; Greek and Seleucid styles became popular in India, and the Indian arts of stone carving and painting embraced the influence of the great artists of the Mediterranean world.

Following centuries of Buddhist domination of all forms of artistic expression, from the fourth century onwards Hinduism was once more ascendant. The Gupta Dynasty, centred on the north Indian plains, instituted the 'Classical' period of India's history. As Buddhism declined the Hindu revival gained confidence and a great era of temple building ensued, steered by the newly revived priestly hierarchy. The image of a god now emerged as the centre of worship rather than sacrifice, a devotional emphasis known as *bhakti*. To assimilate the more popular village and tribal gods and win their followers, orthodox Hinduism created a variety of avatars, or tangible incarnations, of the principal deities. The Hindu craftsman was also guided: early in the tenth century his role was defined in the thirty-two manuals of the Shilpashastra, which formalized the ethics of design and the social stratification of the artisans. The outpouring of creative achievement is powerfully evident in the temple complexes of India, constructed between the fifth and the sixteenth centuries by the combined talents of architects, sculptors and uncounted devoted workmen and women.

These Hindu temples were built as the centre of the religious, social and economic life of the community, and their layout brilliantly succeeds in combining interior and exterior function. On entering the portals of a temple and walking around the complex, one finds oneself a part of a vital harmony given substance by the interlocking rhythmical system of measurements in the buildings, all perfect in proportion and order. The proliferation of stone carved deities in a host of manifestations sets up associations in the mind of the devotee who, on reaching the inner sanctum where the principal deity resides, moves closer to the veneration of the supreme absolute and experiences a moment of salvation. For the non-Hindu used to quiet contemplation, it is often difficult to discern how to entertain such thoughts in a temple complex which is seldom silent. To mark the comings and goings of the faithful bells are sounded with vigour; worshippers prostrate themselves among the throng; and offerings of fruit, vegetables and money are made to the deity and priests alike. In no other religious centre can there be such a free expression of emotion as in a Hindu temple.

This thriving cult of a multitude of gods and goddesses was challenged, again from over the mountains of the north and north-west, as successive waves of Central Asian and Persian raiders and invaders poured in, forcibly converting their conquests to their own Islamic faith. The first of these raids swept out of

Northern India has witnessed the birth, or adoption, of a series of religions during its history. Whereas Hinduism came with the Aryan settlers from afar, and Islam by way of the Arab merchants and Central Asian conquerors, the Buddhist, Jain and Sikh beliefs are original to India. Buddhism once united much of the country, spreading north and east beyond the Himalayas to the Orient. Today, it is confined to some 5 million peoples of India, especially in Ladakh, where the monastery of Shey houses this impressive statue of Buddha (opposite).

By comparison, Hinduism forms the religion of the majority in India. Its pantheon of gods and goddesses offers considerable scope for the creation of colourfully caparisoned temple effigies, typified by these representations of Krishna and his consort Radha (above). Away from the hubbub surrounding such deities, many a Hindu temple such as the Radhamadhav temple at Vrindaban, Uttar Pradesh (left), is also a place of peace and calm.

Of all the holy cities of India, Benares (Varanasi) most memorably encapsulates the power of religious beliefs across the land. Many Hindus make their final pilgrimage to this metropolis on the Ganges, seeking an auspicious site to end their days; others come to bathe in, and make offerings to, this most holy of rivers. Fronting the Ganges are the many ghats, or stepped embankments, that are always teeming with devotees and traders, such as this flower seller (above), or the washermen and women (right), whose vigorous pounding echoes across the water from first light. Benares is not only a centre for Hindus, however; past Muslim conquest is evident in the mosques built of stone from desecrated Hindu temples, such as Aurangzeb's mosque (opposite).

Afghanistan in AD 998, eventually leading to the establishment of the Delhi Sultanate in 1192. This regime was succeeded in the sixteenth century by another group of adventurers from beyond the mountains, the direct descendants of Tamerlane and Genghis Khan, who founded a dynasty that was to rule the magnificent and legendary Mughal empire. For over 500 years, therefore, Islam held sway over northern India, a period of exciting cultural change. Travellers and artisans from all over the Islamic world – which stretched from Portugal to Bengal – came and went, some remaining to add yet another layer to the demographic mix and architectural variety of north India. Although the Hindus remained in the majority, the converts to Islam were many, especially from the lower Hindu castes seeking to improve their lot, and from the Buddhists, who could adapt more readily to such a strict and formal religion.

Craftsmen of all faiths, however, worked together to build the mosques, tombs, palaces and edifices so beloved of the Central Asian Muslims. From far and wide, from towns and villages, craftsmen were drawn to the court and its urban surroundings, and a new era of regal patronage began. There is no doubt that this court industry had a profound effect on the nature of craft

production beyond the towns and cities; for the provincial aristocracy and the wealthy eagerly sought to mimic the style of their exotic new rulers. Mughal patronage was of a particularly sensitive and fruitful nature. Craftsmen, architects and builders were attracted to the empire from all over Asia. Court workshops sought to improve on the best of the existing Sultanate and traditional Persian achievements; what we now view as Mughal arts and habits – miniature painting, the characteristic architecture and formal dress, the love of poetry and social etiquette – all have roots in this refined synthesis, blended by the brilliant interpretative skills of Indian culture. Such an atmosphere of adaptability, imitation and technical excellence continues today to pervade the arts and crafts of the region. Fine silk brocades and woollen weaves and embroidery have made Benares (Varanasi) and Kashmir renowned the world over; Agra continues to be a centre for the carving and decorating of marble and other stone; and Delhi maintains its position as a city of workshops practising crafts from all over the country, a precedent established by the whims of the Mughal court and now put to good use to meet the rapidly changing demands of the tourist and exporter.

In a region so richly endowed with layer upon layer of beliefs and customs, it is no wonder that the towns and cities are a repository of history as well as of living energy. Northern Indian cities such as Delhi, Lucknow, Agra, Mathura and Benares are studded with the buildings and architectural remains of the Hindu, Buddhist and Muslim faiths. Of these, Benares holds the greatest allure for the visitor, demonstrating with dramatic intensity the truly Indian mixture of old and new, life and death, beauty and squalor. The dynamic nature of the city and its environs, even by the frenetic standards of India, is astonishing. As a centre of learning the city university is internationally renowned; for bustle and colour the lanes of traders and shopkeepers is ever exhilarating. The view of the Ganges flowing tirelessly by provides a moment of calm that must have soothed the hearts and minds of millions of pilgrims over the centuries. Benares, known to Hindus as Kashi or City of Light, is one of the oldest cities on earth. Now, as every day for thousands of years, multitudes of pilgrims throng to the place on the sacred Ganges where the Hindu god Shiva has dwelt since creation. Repeated sackings by the Muslims since the twelfth century have ensured that very little of Benares is more than 500 years old. The heart of the city runs to a timeless beat, however, and a walk down any of the narrow, twisting and winding lanes, past one of the 2000 or more temples on the way to the bathing *ghats* that line the west bank of the river, remains a fascinating, exciting and moving experience.

THE FESTIVAL OF DIWALI

This celebration, also known as Deepavali, the Festival of Lamps, takes place each year on a moonless night at the end of October or the beginning of November. Although practised all over India, it is followed with energy in the northern states and especially by the merchant communities as it marks the new financial year.

For weeks beforehand, there is much preparation. Diwali is a festival in honour of Lakshmi, the goddess of wealth and prosperity, who is thought to enter and bless only the homes that are clean and well maintained. Houses, shops and offices are swept, dusted and scrubbed, and the walls painted or whitewashed with zeal. Families seek to be united on this day, and make ready by rolling wicks for the simple clay oil lamps and arranging a supply of delicious sweetmeats (above right) as celebratory gifts for friends and relatives.

On the evening of the day itself, homage to Lakshmi is made within the family temple with offerings of fruit and flowers; auspicious designs (below right), known as rangoli, are drawn on the floor by the women of the household. As darkness falls, the devotional lamps are lit. Set in neat rows along wall, parapet, window ledge and verandah in almost every household, the myriad of flickering flames creates a remarkable spectacle.

THE FESTIVAL OF HOLI

Whereas Diwali heralds the onset of the winter season, Holi is the festival of spring, and is celebrated in a riotous manner. For two or three days in February or March, particularly in northern India, it is unwise to travel, for young and old, rich and poor alike are likely to be showered with coloured water or powder.

At Holi time all is forgiven and much forgotten in an orgy of dancing and drum-playing, the participants smeared with colour on clothes, face and body. Holi is associated with Lord Shiva and commemorates his marriage procession, reflected in the noisy parades that wind through the streets, often culminating in a late evening bonfire.

Throughout northern and central India Holi is celebrated in a multitude of ways. The most dramatic rituals occur in the settlements around Mathura and Vrindaban in Uttar Pradesh, the centres of Krishna worship. In Nandgaon, the village of Krishna's birth, the temple is packed for a celebration of the spring harvest, during which coloured powders and dyed water are thrown from the overhead balcony onto the throng below (overleaf). At Barsana, home of Krishna's consort Radha, the men are beaten with sticks by their womenfolk in a unique moment of role reversal; this elder (opposite) has bandaged his head to protect himself from their chastising blows.

THE EAST

Just beyond the thriving market town of Madhubani there lies, in a thicket of acacia scrub, the *kumbhar* or potters' enclave of the locality. Deep in this remote district of north-central Bihar in eastern India, generations of Hindu potters have faithfully served the rural community, son following father in his profession, their meagre living mirroring the fortunes of their predominantly farming clientèle. So integral to the livelihood of the community is the potter that, until recently, payment for services was always made in kind, bartering pots and terracotta items for the use or the produce of the land.

Each day, as ever, the potter rises and begins work according to the rhythms of the season. During the monsoon months the wheel stands at rest against the hut wall and the farm smallholding is tended; after the rains it is spun daily with gusto, its master eager to supply the neighbourhood with water pots, food containers, festival lamps, idols and cooking vessels. We arrived at his home shortly before Diwali, the Festival of Lamps, for which the potter had been busily throwing small clay lamps since dawn, keen to benefit from the cool and humid conditions of the early morning. Calm and gentle, unruffled by our presence, the potter took another slab of clay, centred his work on the wheel, and with practised ease summoned up another shape from the inert earth. Beside him on the ground, all around his solid stone wheel, were the pleasing fruits of his labour: row upon row of near-identical small round clay saucers, drying in the shade, ready to be stacked as a self-contained pyramid kiln composed of terracotta interleaved with the fuel of cow-dung cakes, sticks of wood, sawdust and straw.

Journeying by rail from Benares through Bihar and into West Bengal over the Gangetic flatlands, one is overwhelmed by the continuous presence of humanity. Village after village merges into an interminable string of habitation, circling the vortex of energy that is the sprawling city of Calcutta. Away from the Westernized sophistication of the urban centres, however, life in these rural districts remains unperturbed by the outside world. The basketmakers and potters create forms that would be familiar to their ancestors, and the weavers still produce muslins of the finest quality, renowned in Roman times as being 'as fine as the slough of a snake, in which the yarn cannot be seen'.

As a timeless fount of creative achievement in its simplest and most sincere form, the work of the village craftsman such as the Bihari potter proved a powerful inspiration for Mahatma Gandhi. Burdened by the dumping of mass-produced goods from British

Little visited by either foreign or indigenous travellers are the lands of Bihar, which harbour thriving communities of craftsmen and women, typified by this potter (opposite below), seen preparing lamps for the festival of Diwali. The region of Mithila is renowned for its enclave of painters who dwell in or around the village of Madhubani. Their walls are gaily decorated with all manner of scenes from local folklore as well as Hindu mythology. Here, the goddess Durga deals a deadly blow to the buffalo demon (opposite above).

The eastern states of India, which border the Ganges as it flows to the Bay of Bengal, are packed with densely populated rural communities that seemingly coalesce into one continuous ribbon of villages. Farmers jostle for the grazing of the common pastures and it is not unusual to see each buffalo or cow tended by a child, often asleep amidst the contours of the ruminant's back.

In the heartland of Bihar the end of the monsoon sees the successful conclusion to a day's foraging for goat and owner alike (above).

factories from the mid-nineteenth century onwards, the creative heart of the nation, its craftspeople, was being poisoned by trade in the mediocre, and the minds of the people were polluted by the mimicry of European culture. Seeking to reawaken a sense of national, cultural and social pride, Gandhi chose to highlight and promote the merits of India's indigenous craftwork, and particularly the making and wearing of the hand-spun and woven cloth known as *khadi*. By encouraging a return to self-sufficiency for town dweller and villager alike, Gandhi looked to create a renewed sense of national identity and independent self-respect. In turn, this movement inspired the post-independence interest in handicrafts and the setting up of the All-India Handicrafts Board in 1948. This created state emporia to market handicrafts, offering commercial incentive to the village and town artisan. Criticism that standards of excellence were being neglected led, from 1965, to the annual presentation of national awards and cash gifts to master craftsmen and women of exceptional skill and imagination.

DURGA PUJA FESTIVAL

Each year, in either September or October, the festival of Durga Puja is celebrated in the eastern states, in particular West Bengal. In this commemoration and representation of the victory of the goddess Durga over the buffalo demon, the citizens of Calcutta excel. Districts of the teeming city vie with each other to build the most spectacular and original temporary pandals of bamboo and cloth (opposite) within the parks to shelter the effigies of the goddess (left). These life-size models are made of straw, and then coated with clay (above) and coloured with many layers of paint. The city of Calcutta is transformed by the preparations for this event which culminates in the transportation of the deity to the banks of the Ganges, where yet more celebrations are conducted before the final immersion of the effigy in the holy waters.

The peoples of southern India enjoy a separate history and culture to those in the north. This is a land of magnificent Hindu sanctuaries such as the Meenakashi temple at Madurai, Tamil Nadu (right), whose high-rise gopurams, or gate towers, look down over this expanding town. The coastal enclave of Mahabalipuram is similarly well endowed with the architectural and craft skills of the past, which provide inspiration for the craftsmen of the present. Behind the bas-relief known as Arjuna's Penance lie a series of rock-cut cave temples (above). In tropical Kerala a fisherman poles through the backwaters south of Cochin in his handcarved boat (opposite).

THE SOUTH

We approached the village of Swamimalai, east of Thanjavur, along a palm-shaded road on the river levee, enjoying the peaceful view of the Cauvery delta countryside. This district of central-eastern Tamil Nadu in southern India is renowned for its bronze casters, and the revered status of these craftsmen ensured that our recommended artist was easily found. Surrounded by paddies of brilliant green puddled with abundant river water, his house with its garden was a refined and comfortable abode. Here again was a craftsman following the family lineage of his art; yet for over a thousand years their patronage has been of an elevated nature, stemming from kings and priests.

The artistic inheritance of these craftsmen enjoys a long and distinguished history, springing from the dynamism of the early Graeco-Buddhist influences, encouraged by the confidence of the Gupta and Classical Indian styles, active despite the uncertainty of the medieval period and in decline under the rule of the British. Currently the work of these sculptors in bronze is undergoing a successful if introspective renaissance. Now, however, rather than working in obsequious deference to a feudal master, executing temple and palace commissions, many of these artists in metal enjoy both their hereditary high status and the financial rewards of the national and international art market. The best of their work is directed towards the excellent reproductions of Chola and Classical sculptures to the order of specialist dealers and private galleries around the world.

After a sojourn in the northern lands of India, where a hectic history is more than matched by a relentless pace of life in the modern age, a journey to the south is a happy respite. Separated from the rest of India by the Vindhya mountains, the states of Andhra Pradesh, Tamil Nadu, Kerala and Karnataka possess an altogether different yet equally diverse range of cultures, climate and topography. Unlike most of India, much of the south enjoys two monsoons a year so that in the eastern lands of Tamil Nadu semi-annual harvests of rice and sugar cane are possible. On the mountains and plains of much of the western coast, by contrast, it is simply too wet for rice cultivation, and instead tea, coffee, rubber, hardwoods, spices and coconuts are cultivated. The physical nature of the land is particularly complex so that, for instance, in the region where Andhra Pradesh, Karnataka and Kerala meet, a 200-mile drive may traverse arid, boulder-strewn plateaus, climb temperate mountain ranges and then descend by way of tropical rainforests to rice paddies and waterways that are often bordered by stretches of deserted beach.

Largely protected by these physical barriers from both the ceaseless intrigues of the north and most of its foreign invaders, the south developed over the centuries a series of local Hindu empires that maintained a largely continuous and consistent culture. The Classical period, for instance, lasted until late in the seventeenth century, during which time the merchant guilds of the south established themselves as a powerful commercial and political force across the land. Their gifts and donations, such as the purchase of an entire village for a temple, secured the guilds' support from royalty and state officials, allowing them access to markets anywhere in India. Again in contrast to the north, the guilds maintained much of their status and power until recent times, ensuring that the craftsmen of the south were well supported by a constant flow of commissions. Such was the confidence of the southern lands that the sculpture and architecture of the time remains unparalleled in the history of the arts of Hinduism. The magnificent temples of Madurai and Tanjore, for example, are covered with sculptured stone images and decoration, from the exterior to interior columns, brackets and ceilings, while their inner shrines guard exquisite bronzes of deities, donors and saints made by the lost wax process.

pintado and the floral chintz, which furnished the drawing rooms of seventeenth-century Europe. Today the weaving and dyeing of the deeply coloured silks long associated with the saris, the traditional unstitched dress of southern Indian women, attract many a foreign buyer to the textile merchants of Karnataka and Tamil Nadu.

Thanks to the diverse origins of the many visitors to the southern coastal lands of India over the ages, religious beliefs in the south are also extraordinarily varied. Jews, Christians and Muslims, Arabs, Chinese, Portuguese, Dutch, French and English came and went, all leaving in their wake influences that still abound in the robust, open-minded and extrovert culture of the south. Driving through the back roads of Tamil Nadu or Kerala, for instance, it is not unusual to chance upon a Hindu temple, a Roman Catholic church and a mosque vying for the souls of one small community. In a style that matches their culture, vivacious invocations and pictorial allegiances are evident on the roads throughout southern India. Moving billboards for the faithful, painted lorries, carts and rickshaws depict an endless and colourful variety of scenes from the Ramayana, the New Testament and the Koran, as well as more secular items such as political slogans, film-star heroes and heroines and portrayals of local landscapes. The trucks of Kerala are particularly well decorated, so that scarcely a scrap of metalwork, from bumper to cab roof, is left unadorned.

Just as such vehicles and the attitudes of their drivers are a striking visual manifestation of the more colourful and easygoing way of life found in the south, so the life of the craftsmen and women of town and village is often in pleasing contrast to that in other regions of India. In a region little visited by tourists, the welcome accorded to the visitor to the workshop or home of a craftsman is one of affable courtesy that is liberally embellished with a genuine desire to share in the joy of creating. This even temperament has been much encouraged by the continuity in purpose and content of such crafts; for it is, on the whole, rare to find a craftsman working to the requirements of a foreign interpretation of a traditional Indian art form. The indigenous market maintained by the millions of pilgrims who flock throughout the year to the temple centres of the south, as well as the needs of the densely populated local hinterland, ensures that the forms of Hindu deities instituted in antiquity still remain in great demand today. The consummate ease with which the craftsman's skilled hands work the chisel across the wood or metal to form elegantly poised figures typifies the pride that the southern Indians take in their contributions to the arts and crafts of the nation, for their fingers are guided by the centuries-old traditions of their ancestors.

Whereas the southern region has been largely untouched by the physically disruptive invasions of the Muslims, the area has not been immune to the influences of foreign trade over the millennia. Carried by Arab dhow or local coastal barque the textiles, jewellery, sculpture, metalwork, precious woods, dyestuffs and spices flowed from the southern lands to Southeast Asia, China, Africa, and via the Mediterranean into the trading ports of Europe. For thousands of years the lure of these valuable objects and exotic raw materials has drawn seaborne traders, exiles and adventurers to the Coromandel and Malabar coasts. As elsewhere in India, the ingenuity and adaptability of the craftsmen in meeting the needs of an export market were in evidence from an early date. At the Roman settlement of Arikamedu near Pondicherry on the Tamil Nadu coast a specialized export production evolved in which specific colours and patterns of muslins were woven to meet the changing fashionable requirements of the Mediterranean consumer some 4000 miles distant. In later centuries these textile traditions of the south are well remembered for the printed and painted export cloths, the

The exotic contrasts between north and south India extend beyond the realms of temple architecture, food, climate and dress. The highways are dominated by the wayward antics of the truck drivers, as anywhere in India, but the lorries of Kerala (opposite) seem less aggressive, painted with peaceful pastoral scenes and representations of gods and goddesses of all denominations.

The women of the south enjoy considerably more personal freedom than their counterparts further north. Here, a woman is carving sweetmeat moulds out of wood in Mysore, Karnataka (above). During the harvest festival of Pongal, women share the task of pounding the freshly harvested rice (right) that will be sprinkled on the ground that evening to form auspicious threshold decorations, known as kolams.

WOOD AND STONE

ARCHITECTURAL CARVING

The old buildings of India contain a feast of inspiration for today's craftsmen in wood and stone. The erstwhile merchants of Jaisalmer in Rajasthan lavished carved decoration on their sandstone havelis (left). In the south, such artisans were traditionally supported by temple-building projects, as seen at Vellore, Tamil Nadu.

The technique of carving is one of humanity's earliest creative expressions. Armed with a stone blade, the simple hunter-gatherers of the Indian forests in prehistoric times would have cut and hewn wood, gradually progressing to the more advanced skills of chiselling and turning, carving and incising. Craftsmen in wood and stone, practitioners of what have been the essential crafts of construction throughout successive empires, enjoy similar ranks within the caste system, testifying to an early respect for their services. The *kammalan* communities of southern India comprise élite groups of five high-caste artisans that embrace both wood carvers, holding the onomatopoeic title of *tac'chan*, and stonemasons, with the even more percussive name of *kal-tac'chan*. Members of this community are able to trace their ancestry back to the five sons of the god of the arts, Viswarkarma; the second-born son, Maya, worked in wood, and the fourth, Silpi, in stone. Similarly, in the north of India, both groups of craftsmen are closely linked by intermarriage and are now often ranked together as *sutradhars*, or 'holders of the line or rein' – a particular reference to the strategic importance of the woodworker from Aryan times as builder and driver of the horsedrawn vehicle of war, the chariot.

THE WOOD CARVER

Classical texts describe the way in which woodworkers, key members of the community, were organized. Formal instructions and guidelines helped to preserve the environment and maintained the quality of their work. The auspicious nature or otherwise of certain trees and the suitability of their situation is given very clearly in the Matsya Purana:

The wood of the *bo* tree and other milky trees should not be used for a building; nor should the wood of trees inhabited by a large number of birds or one burnt up by fire be used. ... The wood of trees broken by elephants, struck by lightning, half dried up or dried up of itself, or those growing near a *chaitya* [shrine] or sacrificial place, temple, confluence of two rivers, burial ground, well or tank, should in no case be used for house building.

This scripture also encourages the householder to have a door frame of carved wood, signifying the threshold and a welcoming entrance to guests. The elaborate carved door frames, balconies and beam ends with their associated brackets formed of animals, birds and human forms seen throughout India in simple homes, palaces and temples are a testament to this prescription.

An early sixth-century text, the Brihatsamhitha by Varahamihira, also elaborates on the sanctity of wood, specifying the type and use of trees, those to be used for icons as opposed to those for house building; it also guides the craftsmen in the rites and ceremonies to be performed before and during the creative act. Later texts, such as the Tamil Mayamatha of the tenth century, instructed the craftsmen who were to achieve the great works of the Chola empire; likewise, the eleventh-century treatise on art and architecture, the Shilpashastra, informed and continues to inform the technique of the Indian woodworker – including advice on how and when to cut the tree in order to propitiate the tree spirits, and the recognized proportions for a particular sculpture.

Among the general community of woodworkers there has developed a hierarchy of work. Those engaged in commonplace tasks such as building construction, the manufacture of household utensils and the making of agricultural tools have a lower rank. These carpenters, known as *thachar aachaari* in the south, would if necessary serve under a master craftsman, or *sthapathi*, on a major project such as a temple or palace, the latter ensuring that work was carried out according to the religious texts. Such has been the shortage of patronage for grand schemes, however, that this division has been confused over the past two centuries.

Encouraged by government policy to educate a wider social range of apprentices, and seeking whatever work is available, these craftsmen can no longer specialize as before. Competent artisans of all backgrounds now turn their tools to the production of culturally degenerate forms such as popular European-style furniture, decorative idols, boxes and trinkets. Many, in this their dark age of creative incentive, retain historical titles with pride and, especially in the south, continue to mix their more mundane work with the temple commissions that come to their workshops by virtue of generations of faithful service. But for all Indian woodworkers more immediate and pressing concerns cloud the future. All around, from high mountain slopes to tropical paddy fields, the pressure of rising population has denuded the land of forest and grove, forcing the government to restrict felling. As a scarce and dwindling resource, wood is now expensive, encouraging the use of other materials and bringing further decline to these workers, the first of the empire-building craftsmen.

India's woodworkers, from select temple craftsmen to village cart makers, continue to work in the style of their ancestors with the simplest of tools. For a mallet, a rectangular block of the hardest wood to hand will suffice. Carving implements are easily sharpened and replaced, being no more than a collection of flats of steel or iron, their blades or points ground on the premises, or by the local blacksmith. Measurement is a matter of judgement and experience: a rule is seldom seen and a tape measure virtually unknown. As in other crafts, work is undertaken on the ground; bench and vice are superfluous as a dextrous pair of feet provides a secure grip on the object. Larger commissions are carved standing up, if necessary on site. Drilling is usually for surface decoration only and is done with a bow drill; a bow is also used to power the lathe for turning components. In the workshops of the towns and cities an electric motor has tended to replace human power, driving a group of lathes through a series of slapping and whirring canvas bands.

WOOD CARVING FOR THE HOME

Many a doorpost would once have been embellished with carved figures and motifs for visual delight as well as a religious boon. An old wooden gateway in Puri, Orissa, has been carved with the scene of a young woman offering up a lighted lamp as an act of respectful worship (above right). In Jaisalmer, Rajasthan, elaborately carved stonework is complemented by sturdy yet decorative wooden doors (right).

For the most part, the more recent style of construction for urban dwellings has followed a less traditional pattern so that many a craftsman in wood or stone now finds support for his skills in the production of artefacts. Decorative panels, such as this teak wood scene (left) of Krishna teasing his milkmaids, from Andhra Pradesh, are now popular throughout India.

The techniques of carving wood are essentially five-fold. Freestanding icons, human and animal figures are carved in the round from a large block of wood. Flat surfaces, such as decorative panels and door lintels, may be decorated in high or low relief, where the background is cut away to leave the subject raised. For smaller ornamental and decorative work, chip carving is common, while incised carving, done freehand without preliminary drawing, is suited to the manufacture of flower and creeper traceries. For the most dramatic ornamentation pierced carving is used, a highly demanding technique as all but the elements of the design itself must be cut away.

Despite the general decline of woodworking, the states of Kashmir, Gujarat, Tamil Nadu, Kerala and Karnataka contain enclaves of master craftsmen. However, finding the artisans at work on a traditional commission is not commonplace. Near Thanjavur, on one of the more peaceful roads in Tamil Nadu, one such workshop endeavours to maintain a living through work for the temple and discerning patrons. Situated in a shaded compound just off the street, the cool, dark interior of the workshop houses an array of large freestanding wooden sculptures of birds. These mythical swans and peacocks are processional mounts, known as *vahanas*, for the deity, and represent today's vestiges of the high eloquence of Tamil temple carving. Seated by the unfinished peacock and following a rough chalk outline on a panel between his feet, the master craftsman works the chisel over the wing of a bird with relaxed assuredness. As he looks up to converse, there is no pause in the deft manipulation of the tools over the wood; yet there is no hurry, and as he works he shares, with all the generosity and stature of his years, memories of his family's craft over the generations. In addition to the swan and peacock mounts they also create the processional cars, or *thers*. These mobile shrines and platforms for the temple deity are set on four or more massive, shield-like solid wheels. Up to eight metres of tiered wood side panels, their carving relating to the stone sculpture and friezes of the associated temple, lead up to the plinth. A cohort of deities and a fantastic zoo of mythical and realistic animals, set in a garden of floral and trellis work, are carved in high relief. Height and colour are emphasized by the cloth-decked wooden structure that rises from the platform. On this plinth stand the charioteer, his horses and guardians, and above them the festival deity, the *uthsavam*, rides in jewelled and floral splendour on the topmost platform. As large as an elephant or even an ocean-going yacht, these highly decorated cars are pulled by devotees through the streets of the town or village.

But even a workshop such as this cannot live by temple work alone. Clearly the past is being adapted to the present. Planks

TEMPLE CARVINGS OF SOUTH INDIA

For the fortunate few, and especially in the south, there are the rare commissions from the temple to execute. In a workshop near Thanjavur, Tamil Nadu, a master craftsman in wood carves and assembles a vahana, *or processional vehicle for a deity (previous page). The more mundane orders, such as cupboard doors, display the same time-honoured virtuoso skills.*

TEMPLE CARS OF SOUTH INDIA

In Tamil Nadu wooden temple art is now a dying craft. Major sanctuaries, however, still have their temple cars, or thers, *that can reach massive proportions, here seen dwarfing the resting pilgrims at Tirumalai, Andhra Pradesh (opposite). These wooden cars are carved with a multitude of panels (above) depicting a host of deities, as well as animal and floral motifs.*

template out of sheet spruce; these pieces, forming a splendid wooden jigsaw, are held in place by borders of grooved battens. Seen in the cabins of the large houseboats as well as within dwellings on land, this joinery technique is matched by the marvellous *pinjra* latticed panel work. Extremely thin laths of deodar wood, a variety of cedar, are latticed together to form architectural panels, the springiness of the wood maintaining their integrity largely without fixings. These older practices have now been overshadowed by the more portable tourist craft of walnut carving, which was encouraged by European traders at the end of the nineteenth century. The rich, dark and robust wood is an ideal medium for intricate carving and undercutting, and is made into elaborately worked lamps, boxes, table tops and screens. Some of this Kashmiri woodwork deserves admiration for its virtuoso carving alone.

Farther down the valley villages such as Anantnag and Kulgam supply quantities of turned and carved willow and horse chestnut wood. Ladles, cooking spoons, rolling pins, chapati boards and sandals are produced; most of the lathe work is lacquered in bright colours. The handles of long wooden spoons are often adorned with musically clattering wooden rings, cut in one piece from the shafts on the lathe. Another craft from below the Kashmir Valley in Jammu, and popular since Mughal times, is the carving of fine-toothed double-sided fretwork combs in *chikri* wood. These are especially popular among the women of the Gujjar and Bakarwal tribes. *Chikri* wood resembles ivory, being light in colour and possessing almost no grain. Such carving is practised in the cluster of villages known as Thana Mandi, where the craftsmen are also diversifying into more modern items. Below the Himalayan range, in Uttar Pradesh, is Saharanpur, the principal timber market of India and known nationwide for its large output of furniture, decorative items and utensils in white *dudhi* wood and the heavily grained brown *shisham*. Carving influences from Kashmir are strong among the predominantly Muslim craftsmen of this region. Again in Uttar Pradesh, Farrukhabad is famous for the production of intricate and deeply carved textile printing blocks with elegant floral designs.

From the arid Barmer and Jaisalmer districts of Rajasthan down to the scrub woodland of Saurashtra in Gujarat there extends a swathe of similar wood-carving traditions. The carpentry and carving community of this area is known as the *mistri*. Their ingenious designs and skilled execution are evident in the extensive range of decorated artefacts which they produce, as well as in their architectural fantasies. The more historic work is seen in the old palaces, *havelis* or merchants' mansions, and farmhouses of the region. Wood is exquisitely carved in the form of, or decorated with, horses, elephants and parrots; and both

of teak are worked in low relief, inspired by the temple car panelling, as decorative friezes for urban homes in India and abroad. In the same way stolid European-style pieces of furniture are carved with depictions of the god Krishna in a playful pose, a bizarre application of indigenous art. The workshop's most popular artefacts for galleries and export alike are interpretations of the *vahana*, scaled down to fit in the home and 'distressed' by baking in the sun and by the application and repeated removal of layers of paint.

The roads of India now carry hardwoods throughout the land, but certain villages, towns and districts continue to specialize in their ancient craft of carving the local wood. Of these, Kashmir is one of the principal historical centres for fine carving. Abundant stocks of wood enabled the construction of extravagant timber palaces, which were built as early as the eleventh century. The style reached its peak during the sixteenth century in the grandiose overhanging balconies of the palaces of King Zain-ul-Abadin. Many of the houses and houseboats around the canal banks of the Dal and Nagin lakes continue to display the influence of this style. For the commoners, timber house building was made possible by an edict of King Jayasimha in the twelfth century allowing a free supply of forest timber for all.

Kashmir's thousand-year history of popular architectural wood carving and joinery has generated a range of indigenous techniques. In *khatumband* work, intricate geometrically patterned panelled ceilings are created by cutting the components on a

CARVING WOODEN DEITIES, UTENSILS AND TRINKETS

His hands working with deft skill, and using the simplest tools, this village master carver of Andhra Pradesh (opposite) creates the form of the deity Lord Venkateswara, found in the local temple and popular pilgrimage site of Tirumalai.

Seeking to satisfy the needs and demands of a major city, this carver of Mysore, Karnataka (left), is able to turn her hand at a moment's notice from producing teak sugar moulds to decorating a model elephant intended for sale to a visiting tourist.

THE FURNITURE MAKER

The town of Barmer, at the western extremity of Rajasthan, is known for its production of carved wood, printed textiles and embroideries. The royal patrons who once supported fine decorative wood carving no longer exist and today's craftsmen have now become well-known for their furniture-making skills (above).

geometric and floral forms cluster on rafter ends, pillars and brackets, on openwork *jali* screens and windows, and on doors and door frames. Now lacking architectural commissions, the *mistri* craftsmen are engaged in the more mundane construction of European-style beds and furniture; but their traditional skills are still to be seen in the carving, in a precise and shallow technique, of the panels of giant metal-mounted dowry chests, swinging cradles and low chairs, as well as a range of household utensils such as laundry beaters, pestles and mortars, spice containers, rolling boards and platters.

Farther south, beyond the Deccan, where large temples have dominated the cultural, social and economic landscape for a thousand years, there is a thriving trade in the carving and sale of wooden icons. Southern Andhra Pradesh attracts hundreds of thousands of temple visitors each year, who come, especially to Tirumalai in the Tirupati district, in search of the deity Lord Venkateswara. Crudely executed images of this god are popular, carved in the fine-grained, deep red wood known as *sanders*, and worked in the villages of the temple hinterland. To the west, the state of Karnataka is famous for sandalwood and rosewood carving. Many of the craftsmen in Mysore, Bangalore, Kumta and Shimoga are proudly aware of their status as members of the Viswarkarma community, tracing a pedigree back to this deity of the arts. Sandalwood's soft texture, honey colouring, fragrant scent and auspicious associations make objects carved in this wood highly popular throughout India. Boxes and caskets of all sizes, decorated in high and low relief, are found, as well as statues of every imaginable figure of the Buddhist, Hindu, Jain or Christian faiths.

Wood inlay was a form of decoration beloved by the Mughals, and their demand encouraged communities of Persian inlay craftsmen to settle in India; one such group, the *petigaras*, resides in the city of Surat, in Gujarat state. Here, and also in Delhi, Mysore, Hoshiarpur in the Punjab, and much of the state of Karnataka, coloured woods, horn and even plastic are set into the carved surfaces of a range of domestic chattels. Another type of inlay work, known as *tarkashi*, utilizes burnished copper or brass wire set in the wood to create fine geometric compositions; this and other floral work in cut sheet metal flourishes at Jaipur in Rajasthan, and at Mainpuri in Uttar Pradesh. As ever, much fine craftsmanship belongs to the past, for example, the large-scale but delicately detailed work on doorways and architectural woodwork, found in such places as the Mysore Palace. Nowadays much of the work is for the wholesalers, the state shops or for export, whether performed in the north by a Muslim working geometric patterns in inlay on teak jewellery boxes, or a Hindu of the south creating elaborate scenes from the Ramayana on a massive rosewood dining table.

For the tribal cultures of India, wood carving continues to provide simple domestic utensils, decoration for doors and doorways in the form of lively zoomorphic figures, and grand totemic sculptures. Amongst the Nagas of the north-east, the homes of the courageous and wealthy are marked by carved wooden pillars and posts, executed in the round and with a coarse finish full of dramatic power that belies their aboriginal status. On such posts, the marks of distinction include carvings of human heads as a memory of bygone glories, of tigers and elephants to demonstrate ferocity and strength, and hornbills and pythons for auspicious protection. Ancestor worship provides another creative impulse for carved wooden pillars and posts of great energy and strength.

WOODEN TOOLS

Despite the fact that many a village will possess a resident or itinerant carpenter, the farmers of India and their wives are always eager to seek out new tools, utensils and trinkets when they visit the local town or attend a regional market. At the famed Nagaur fair this farmer (opposite) is inspecting a new wooden pitchfork with customary caution, whereas the seller of carved and stained wooden combs (above) hopes to attract the eye of the womenfolk. This Rabari shepherd woman (right) from Kutch in Gujarat has already made her purchase of a string-operated wooden milk churner. The dyer and printer of cloth relies on the skills of the wood carver to complete his work. Here, a shelf of carved wooden blocks await use in the workshop of a printer of the much sought after ajrakh cloth (above right).

THE STONEMASON

From the preparation of simple small stone utensils to grandiose temple commissions, there has evolved over the centuries a tradition of stonemasonry that pervades the whole of the Indian subcontinent. Most craftsmen dwell, necessarily, near their source of raw material, though now much stone is carried from region to region by road. In the south the stonemasons or *silpis* are respected members of the high-caste *kammalan* community. In the seventh century AD, at the time of the Pallavas, their ancestors carved a remarkable scene, known as 'Arjuna's Penance', on two enormous rocks at Mahabalipuram in Tamil Nadu. Later, protected and encouraged by the powerful guilds of southern India, the masons were to be the masterful creators of the magnificent stone temples and carvings of the Chola period.

Like their fellow craftsmen the wood carvers, these masons were guided by the early sacred texts of art and architecture such as the Mayamatha and the Shilpashastra, which set out the desired measurements and techniques for sculpting as well as requirements concerning the quality, colour, texture, maturity and even gender of stone. Gender is ascertained by the tonal qualities of a stone; for example, those that sound like the rustling of palm leaves are female.

Seeking to work in close rapport, the quarry workers and the masons were until recently of the same caste, so that from selection at the quarry face to the finished forms there was a continuity of knowledge and dedication. Stone is sought out for texture and line of growth, and ideally should be without flaws such as stains, patches or spots. In the execution of a religious sculpture, the measurements are usually counted in *hastas*, the length from the elbow to the tip of the middle finger; a *hasta* is made up of twenty-four *angulas*. From a central line the figure or form is marked up with charcoal or red chalk, and the sculptor sets to work with a mild steel chisel and hammer. In contrast to wood carving, the action of the chisel on stone should be to peck and not cut; and to prevent fractures and vibration cracks from the repeated blows, the block is worked flat on the ground.

Despite the force needed to free the form within, stone must be handled with care, for it may be riddled with hidden voids and cracks that will destroy the work if the material is stressed.

Working from front to back, often renewing his chisels from the stock prepared each day in the charcoal furnace of the workshop, and sprinkling water on the surface to separate the dust and chips from the image, the mason gradually reveals the sculpture. Whether working for the temple or the tourist, he is

adept at creating a range of gods and heroes from the Puranic scriptures; foreign-inspired forms are unknown. The work is finished by hours of rubbing with various grades of corundum stones, sandpaper, jeweller's rouge or Multani clay. When a temple icon is created, and after the completion of the face, a ceremony known in Tamil Nadu as *nyanonmilan* is performed, whereby the image is invested with the power of sight and the gift of breath, becoming a living entity.

Following in the wake of their great ancestors, most of the stone carvers of the south are concentrated around the major

ARJUNA'S PENANCE

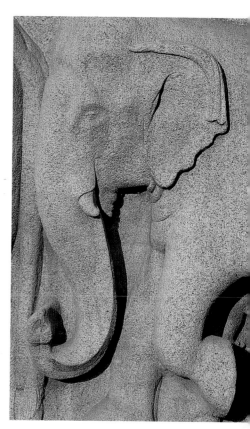

Some forty miles south of Madras lies Mahabalipuram, a city and seaport originally built to provide trading access to Southeast Asia. Once a large and prosperous settlement, Mahabalipuram now attracts visitors from far and wide to view its rock-cut shrines and magnificent shore temple.

Of these, the world's largest bas-relief, known as Arjuna's Penance and the Descent of the Ganges, is an astonishing sight. Carved onto an enormous whale-shaped outcrop of rock during the reign of Narasimha Varman (670–715) is a profusion of delicate and sensitively executed figures and animals dwarfed by lovingly portrayed elephants. The central gaping fissure that divides the relief was once running with water, thus lending credence to the belief that these stone carvings depict Shiva releasing the sacred Ganges from the heavens. Others believe that it depicts the great archer, Arjuna, doing penance in order to persuade the gods to give him an especially powerful bow with which to defeat his enemies.

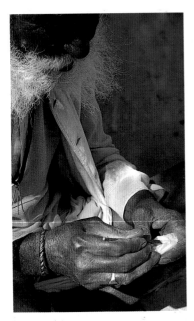

CARVING OF STONE DEITIES

The centres of worship and the
historic sites of India attract not
only pilgrims and tourists, but
also thriving communities of
craftsmen selling commemorative
or auspicious artefacts. Widely
available and easy to carve,
soapstone is always popular;
here, a craftsman from the
pilgrimage town of Nathdwara in
Rajasthan carves one of the
many Hindu deities (above).

The fame of the carved rocks and
stone temples of Mahabalipuram,
Tamil Nadu, has helped to
promote the work of local stone-
carvers. Working in black granite
hauled from Kanchipuram, the
ring of hammers on metal chisels
fills the air from dawn to dusk.
Supplying temples throughout
India with effigies of all sizes,
these craftsmen are here carving
a dancing girl (right) and a
figure of Parvai (opposite above).

temples. Clients for the smaller carvings are numerous and varied. At Puri in Orissa the stonemasons inhabit the Patharasahi quarter, carving replicas of the shore temples in granite and sandstone, as well as icons of all sizes and household utensils. Likewise, the temple village of Mahabalipuram is thronged with craftsmen carving in soapstone and granite; elsewhere in Tamil Nadu the masons flourish in the villages of Salem district such as Thandagoundanpalyam, where soft grey stone food containers are made, as well as in the Kolar district of Karnataka. To the north, the temple traditions survive in the Saurashtra district of Gujarat; at Wadhwan live the *sompura* community of stonemasons, whose ancestors created the Somnath and Dwarka temples as well as the elaborate architectural fixtures that accompany the splendid wood carving of the region.

Away from the areas of temple traditions, masons are most numerous, and perhaps most well known, in the state of Rajasthan. There are districts in Jaipur, Thanagazi, Makrana, Jodhpur, Jaisalmer and Dungarpur that ring throughout the day to the crack of chisels on great blocks of sandstone or marble. For those travelling through these fortress towns and citadels, dotted throughout the lands bordering or within the Thar desert, the renowned craftsmanship of the *silavat* communities of mason is a revelation. Most striking are the architectural features of the large houses, or *havelis*, and the palaces of the region. These homes and follies offer a wealth of surfaces for decoration, with their cool inner courtyards, maze of passageways, high-ceilinged rooms, numerous balconies and roof terraces. Each gateway, balcony, fortification, shutter, screen, lintel, column and frieze is intricately carved with flowing dexterity, attesting to the wealth of the Rajput rulers and their merchant associates between the fourteenth and the nineteenth centuries.

Rising up from the stony desert landscape like a beached galleon, the crenellated citadel of Jaisalmer, built in the twelfth century, is not only a historic site but also a present-day centre of the art of sandstone carving. The approach to the town from the south, along the old caravan road leading all the way from the Arabian Sea, is one of the most memorable sights in all India. As one weaves from sand dune to sand dune, and mounts yet another rocky rise, there suddenly appears in the heat haze of the distance a near-perfect fusion of architecture with landscape.

The descendants of the original builders continue to decorate the new buildings of this growing town in ancestral style. The slabs of yellow sandstone are carried from the local quarries by lorry to a makeshift yard near the construction site, and are split with chisels or cut with a saw into appropriate sizes. The many communities of Muslim stonemasons then go to work in the open, sheltering from the intense sun under a simple cloth shade. Fine

Protected by their isolated rural position, the stone carvers of the village of Patharkatti, Bihar, are renowned for their refined carving of deities, such as this elegant Krishna (left), in local black granite. The ancestors of this community originally practised their trade in Jaipur, Rajasthan, some 350 years ago, and were brought to their present home in order to create the famous black stone Vishnupad Temple in nearby Gaya.

ARCHITECTURAL STONE CARVING

The state of Rajasthan is renowned for the traditional quality and prolific output of its stone masons. Supplied by an abundance and variety of local sandstone and marble, and supported in the past by an extensive network of regal, merchant and religious patrons, the towns of this desert-dominated state are blessed with a fine collection of decorated stone palaces, mansions and temples. Although the finest examples of stone carving and masonry are to be found in early buildings, such as this doorway votive niche (below left), found in a back street of the trading town of Jaisalmer, earnest efforts are now being made by government craft enterprises to encourage the continuation of architectural stone carving practices. An example of such work may be seen on the side of a modern stone house, again in Jaisalmer, which shows the attempted replication of a finely carved wall of jali screens, dominated by a canopied balcony (right). Originally, these fretwork jali screens would have hidden from unsolicited view the antics and inquisitive eyes of the women of the household. Inspired by these screens, slabs of trellis work combining geometric and floral motifs (above left) are carved from the local Jaisalmer sandstone as a popular architectural decoration for the exterior of many a new house in this rapidly expanding town.

work such as *jali*, an ever popular open geometric or floral lattice work, is delicately executed with slender knife-like tools. In the harsh desert landscape where the sun burns with little respite, the *jali* windows, screens and archways create a dappled play of light and shade, at the same time allowing any cooling breeze to pass through.

In Rajasthan, as elsewhere in northern India, the masons also carve personal and household utensils. A hard variety of stone is sought for the carving of the large shallow kneading bowls used for making *parathas*, the small oval kitchen mortars and pestles, and silky-smooth chapati rolling boards. In Bihar such mixed production is carried out at Patharkatti ('the abode of stone cutters'), a village apparently close to the town of Gaya, but in fact only reached by a hard journey on unmade roads which are almost impassable at the end of the monsoon season. The sounds of chisel on stone resonate over the silent paddy fields. This community of some 500 Gaur Brahmans is descended from those craftsmen who were brought hundreds of miles from their Rajasthani homeland in the seventeenth century by the Rani Ahilyabai Holkar, who commissioned them to build the Vishnupad Temple at Gaya in the local black granite. At the finish of the project the group were given a hill of such stone, and encouraged to settle. Separated by status and origin from their neighbouring farmers, and the *harijan* community of the village who emulate their work, these Brahmans inhabit a solitary island of Rajasthani culture. Their work continues the accomplished style of their forebears and encompasses the carving of icons in all sizes and postures, as well as the cutting and polishing of magnificent black stone utensils, much in demand for temple worship and by orthodox high-caste families, and the large mortars or *kharals* used by traditional apothecaries.

Elsewhere in India, stone carvers are often found in close proximity to temples, whether by virtue of tradition (their ancestors having been attracted to the site by the prospect of secure employment during the lengthy period of temple construction) or by virtue of the brisk passing trade of tourist and pilgrim alike. The coastal temple enclave of Puri in Orissa is endowed with a community of such stonemasons. There, working with materials that vary from soft yet brittle sandstone to hard granite, the artisans not only fashion replicas of the temples at Konark, Puri and Bhubaneshwar, but also the images of deities in every size and posture. To meet the needs of the local populace, these craftsmen also turn their hand to the production of domestic utensils of all kinds and it is not uncommon to find the maker and seller of carved stone surrounded by a jumble of lively figurines, mixing bowls, soapstone trinkets, grinding stones, pestles, statuary and temple models.

STONE HOUSEHOLD UTENSILS

The grinding of foodstuffs such as pulses, rice and corn is a major preoccupation for the women of the towns and villages of India. Seeds and fruits are rolled or mashed with a pestle and mortar, and large-scale chores are facilitated by the use of a hand rotated grinder. In a village of Rajasthan, a young woman of the Patel caste (opposite above) sends the stone grinding wheel spinning with a vigorous whirl by grasping the finger-worn wooden handle. The task is to grind millet to flour in order to make the unleavened and highly nutritious, if somewhat compact, bread known as rotla. Known locally as a ghatti, this grinder is also used to split pulses. By raising the stone a few millimetres from the base with a wooden wedge, the seed-like pulses are cracked and neatly split before being spun out into the collecting tray.

In order to supply the demand for replacement grinding wheels, some communities of stone masons specialise in their manufacture. Near Mathura in Uttar Pradesh, a stone wheel is laboriously created from a slab of granite with a pair of tapping hammers (left). The flat bowls known as parath, used for mixing and kneading dough, undergo less rigorous use in an Indian household and so are often made of less robust materials such as wood or, as here, sandstone (opposite below).

PAINT

AUSPICIOUS IMAGERY

In Ladakh, both homes and temples (left) are adorned with all manner of Buddhist iconography. Southwards lie the Gangetic plains of north India, home to farming communities that are steeped in the Hindu faith. This representation (above) from Madhubani in Bihar depicts the universal mother goddess, Devi.

The earliest surviving evidence in India of people's desire to record their life and surroundings is to be seen in the cave paintings of the north, dating from the mesolithic and neolithic eras. Scenes of hunting, dancing and farming have been found scattered at random, suggesting that these paintings enjoyed no ritual significance. Within the village, however, the centuries have witnessed the establishment of painted artistry as a rite and a narrative, rather than mere decoration. Even today, these paintings display a vital, unbroken yet continuously evolving tradition. In contrast, the high Indian culture of painting has its roots in religious institutions and in the monuments of the patrons of the great empires. The earliest of these forms, the exquisite Buddhist frescoes that decorate the walls of the Ajanta caves in western India, are the precursors of the tradition of temple painting in the south. To the north, the culture of painting and ornamentation continued on palm leaves, wood blocks and cloth, and with renewed vigour after the introduction of paper in the twelfth century. The Mughals helped to develop a thriving court tradition of Persian-inspired miniature painting from which sprang many different schools in Rajasthan, the Punjab Hills and central India.

THE PAINTER OF WALLS AND FLOORS

Many a village home in India continues to be painted and ornamented each year according to the historical legacy of the family and community or tribe. Yet the casual visitor walking through the village may never see any evidence of such artistry, for the work is usually confined to the inner courtyard walls or dark interiors. For some communities, such as the Thar desert villages of western Rajasthan, wall and floor painting have evolved into forms which both constitute a decoration and have a sacred and protective role, marking the passage of the seasons. For the former, as a relief to the dun desert and scrub backdrop, the mud and cow-dung plastered walls of their thatched houses are bordered with bands of whitewash that meet at the doorway. There, as a form of welcome and talisman, are auspicious painted forms such as the ancient swastika, an image of the life-giving sun, some lucky parrots and a simple tree of life. These pleasing everyday decorations and symbols are joined at festival time by more sacred paintings, known throughout the region as *mandana*, which are applied to the threshold. They are created daily by the women and girls of the village who draw, with their fingers wrapped in a rag soaked in red paint, the lines that form these protective, auspicious drawings.

Another ephemeral form of visual expression known as *kolam* in the south of India, *rangoli* in Maharashtra, *osa* in Orissa, *alpona* in Bengal, *aripana* in Bihar, *sona rakhna* in Uttar Pradesh, *sathiya* in Gujarat, *aripona* in other regions of northern India and *apna* in the western Himalayas, is created by the women and, less often, by the priests of Hindu communities. Such patterns, drawn at the doorway to the home, are usually geometric or floral in nature, and yet may also be seen to contain a myriad of symbolic and directly representational forms. Created on the paths traced by the traffic to, from and by the house, the full resonance of these diagrams may be fully appreciated only when freshly drawn, before they are again returned to the dust of yet another busy day.

At festival time in the villages it is all too easy to be overwhelmed by the energy of this truly living tradition, which has been handed down from mother to daughter since before the arrival of the Aryans. The ancient Sanskrit works on Indian painting describe the worship of the sun god through the drawing of an eight-petalled lotus flower, or a simple circle, on the ground. In fact these works are but an early sanctioning of the pre-Hindu origins of this form of painting, rooted in ancient animist faiths, which used such diagrams to contain and direct the power of the supernatural. Now, as then, daughters are imbued with the

magic and the spirit of these rice paste or powder drawings from a very early age, beginning to mimic and practice their own versions when only four or five years old, and reaching competence before becoming teenagers. They are able to express in these flowing forms their wishes and desires for this life when taking a *vrata*, or vow.

In some regions, particularly the south, these protective charms are executed daily or twice daily, at dawn and again at dusk, throughout the year; in others, the ritual takes place exclusively at the time of important festivals. The diagrams are also drawn at the passage of one state of life to another, such as at the birth of a child, a boy's investiture with the sacred thread, or a marriage. For many of the women the most important work continues, however, to be the *alpona vrata*, drawn during the winter months and culminating in an epic pictogram at the end of the

WALL AND FLOOR PAINTERS OF MADHUBANI, BIHAR

Of all the wall and floor painters of India, the women of Madhubani are the most celebrated. An ancient medium of expression, the preparation of the newly harvested rice paste (below) and the finger daubing of the designs upon the floor (left) are thought to conjure up the protective powers of the gods. On the hand-rubbed mud wall of the house, scenes from the Hindu epics as well as local tales and auspicious birds and beasts are depicted in a lively and realistic fashion. Working with a twig and paints derived from local plants and seeds, this painter decorates her verandah with an image of a heavenly peacock (opposite).

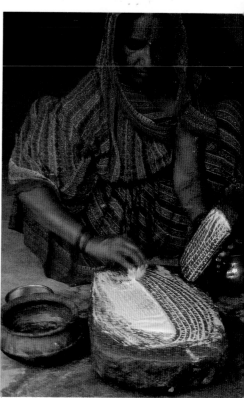

RAJASTHANI WALL PAINTING

The painting of household walls is a vibrant, lively and seasonal activity throughout India. In Shiu village, Rajasthan (right), the dun and dusty landscapes of the Thar desert all around are relieved by the whitewashed patterns and colouring of their mud houses and courtyards. Doorways, gateways and openings in general are the centre of the painter's attention, and as a sign of welcome and respect for the visiting deities as well as the more frequent mortal visitors, auspicious floral as well as geometric patterns are painted on the mud, often in mimicry of stone or wooden structures.

Painted by the women to celebrate a wedding or to mark an annual festival such as Diwali, these wall decorations (left) within a Patel farming household are a folk art form known as mandana in Rajasthan. Their patterns and colours serve not only to decorate but also to represent the aspirations and achievements of the whole family. The common theme of the tree of life is here found rising up from the dry earth in celebration of god's fruitfulness. Fading under the intense glare of the summer sun and washed away by the following monsoon, these mandana will be renewed afresh each year in a constant cycle that echoes the annual hardship, struggles and rewards of work in a village of northern India.

season. A vivid account of *alpona vrata* from a village in Bengal captures the essence of this pictorial tradition:

She kept handfuls of rice of a very fine quality – the *shali* – under water until they were thoroughly softened. Then she washed them carefully and pressed them on a stone. She prepared a white liquid paste with them and first of all she drew the adored feet of her parents who were always uppermost in her mind. She drew two granaries, taking care to paint the footsteps of the harvest goddess in the paths leading to them, and she introduced at intervals fine ears of rice drooping low with their burden. Then she drew the palace of the great god Shiva and his consort Parvati on the Kailasa mountain. In the middle of a big lotus leaf, she painted Vishnu and Lakshmi seated together and on a chariot drawn by the royal swan, she painted the figure of Manasa Devi from whom all victories proceeded. Then she drew the figures of the *siddhas*, who could perform tantric practices, and then those of the nymphs of heaven. She drew a grove of trees and under it the figure of Bani Devi, the silvan deity. Then she painted Raksha Kali, the goddess who saves us from all dangers. The warrior god Karthikeya and the literary god Ganesh she drew next with their respective *vahanas* or the animals they rode. And then Rama and Sita and Lakshmana were drawn by her admirably. She next painted the sea, the sun, and the moon, and the gods Yama and Indra were also introduced into the panorama. And when she had finished, she kindled a lamp fed by sacred butter and then she bowed down with her head bent to the ground.

In the south, particularly in Tamil Nadu, the *kolams* of the harvest festival, known as Pongal, are especially delightful to behold. Here the women draw the outlines of the patterns with freshly harvested rice flour, sifted through thumb and fingers. Bright powder colours, bought in the market, are then sprinkled into each field of the composition as it grows outwards from the centre. Pongal is celebrated during the winter season over three days in honour of Indra, god of the heavens and master of the clouds and rains. It is a time for families to be reunited, for religious vows to be renewed and for pilgrimages to be made. The celebration begins on the last day of the sun's southerly course in the sky, and is known as *bhogi pandigai*, or the festival of physical enjoyment, referring to the happy work of gathering the rice harvest from the paddy fields. On this morning, these stylized patterns of good fortune are dedicated to the sun god, and to welcoming the change of the seasons. All the doorways of the village and town houses alike are ablaze with the radiance of a multitude of colourful circular *kolams*.

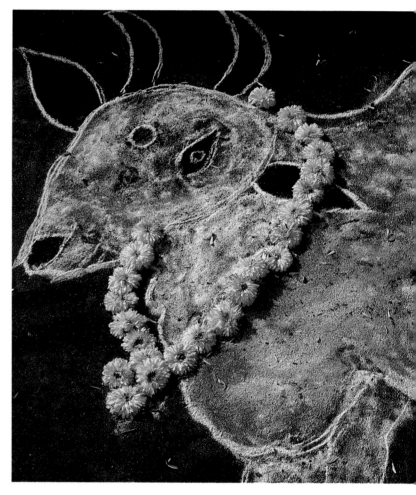

On the night before the second day of the festival the house is thoroughly cleaned and all the accumulated rubbish burnt a good distance away. Before the sun rises to begin its journey into the northern sky, the women are out in the twilight working before their homes to create the *Pongal kolam*. These works realistically depict the feast of Pongal when, outside the home under the rays of the newly emergent sun, the freshly harvested rice, milk and *jaggery* (palm sugar) are cooked in new terracotta pots and offered first to the great luminary, before being eaten with relish by the family.

The third and last day is known as *maatu Pongal*, or Pongal for the cows, when the services of the hardworking cattle are recognized and celebrated with all manner of gaiety and kindnesses. Cows, oxen and buffalo are bathed and decorated with an attentiveness that is both affectionate and gentle. Horns are often tipped with small metal bells and many are painted afresh in contrasting colours. The *kolams* of the day reflect this adoration for the provider of milk and the hardy ox.

FESTIVAL OF PONGAL

For three days each year the threshold of many a household in south India, and particularly in Tamil Nadu, will be decorated with vibrant powder paintings known as kolams. Kolam painting is a common activity throughout the year, but at Pongal, which commemorates the harvest and the return of the sun to the northern hemisphere, the creative ingenuity of the women reaches new heights of expression. Before dawn on the day itself, the artists are seen working with keen diligence to welcome the first rays of the sun that herald a new year. Many a kolam will depict the cooking of a feast (below). More recently, the depiction of secular forms, such as this young girl (right), have proved popular themes but on the last day of the festival the cow is always the centre of attention (left).

A KOLAM FOR PONGAL

Pongal is a time of joy when the riches of the harvest are shared and enjoyed in town and village alike. Drawn with coloured powder, sprinkled between thumb and fingers on the fresh damp earth of the early morning, this kolam of a farmer's wife (overleaf), carrying a load of sugar cane, is from a doorway near Swamimalai, Tamil Nadu, and perfectly captures the spirit of the festivities. Within hours, busy passing feet will obliterate this most ephemeral of painted forms.

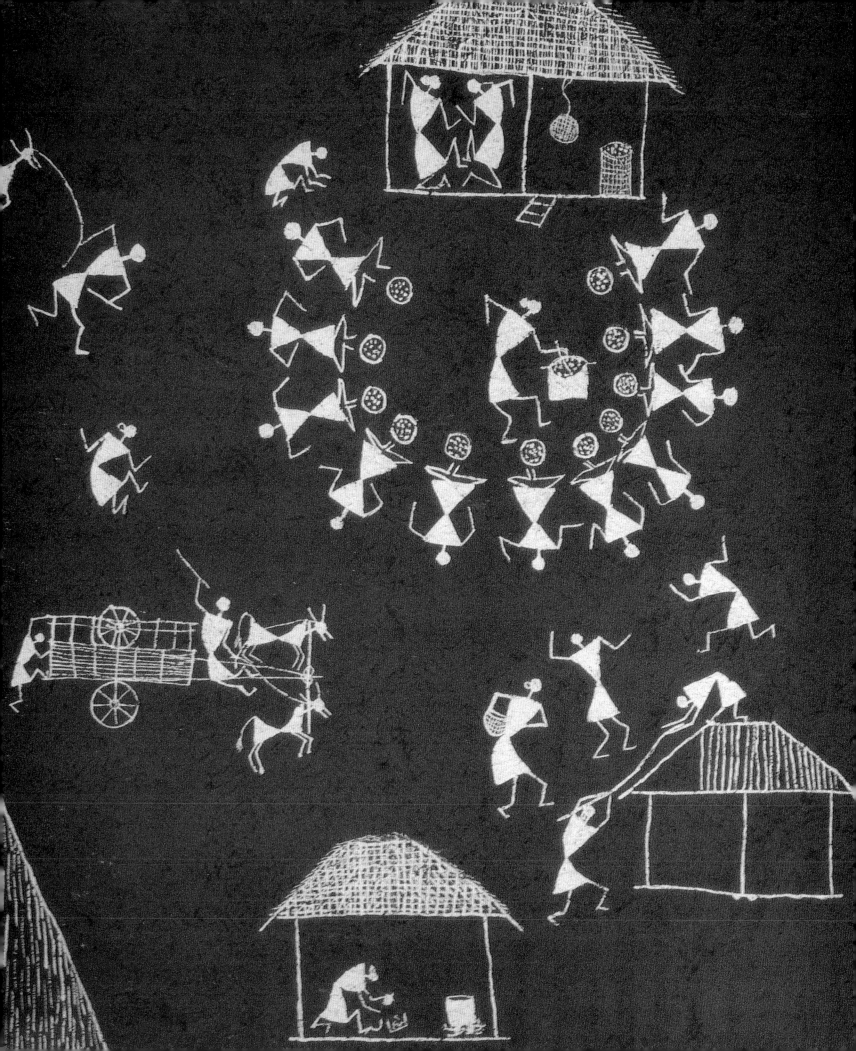

Smaller but no less powerful are the sacred wall paintings of the tribes and village communities of India. There are two principal varieties of such work. The first is seen on the hut walls of the tribal enclaves of Maharashtra, Orissa, Gujarat and Madhya Pradesh; here the paintings have a distinctively primitive style and a strongly pre-Aryan content. The second, that of the Hindu communities of Mithila in Bihar, the coastal districts of Orissa, and Kumaon in Uttar Pradesh, consists of colourful interpretations of the gods and the scriptures that are quite unlike any other Vedic- or Puranic-inspired art in India. Despite their different styles, both types of wall painting are intended to invoke spiritual powers, which are given life by the ritual consecration of the images.

Among the tribal paintings, the work of the Warlis of Maharashtra is a revelation. These white line paintings with their simple, direct and rhythmical execution can be seen as a direct link with the style of their remote ancestors' cave paintings. For the Warlis, life continues to be dominated by the rigours of farming as subsistence smallholders amid the rugged foothills of the Sahyadri range in the district of Thane. This is no easy task, and their one meagre crop a year must be supplemented by hard casual labour in the summer months.

For the Warlis their frugal existence is made possible by the ministrations of the mother goddess Palghat. As purveyor of the bounty of nature, Palghat is also invoked for the continued fertility of mankind, especially at the time of marriage. In their role as the creative rite in the cycle of life, marriages follow the seasons, taking place in February or March. This is the time of the year when the earth is resting, preparing to receive the onslaught of the heat and the life-giving torrents of monsoon rain. And so, to conjure up the merciful bounty of Palghat, the interior wall of the wedding hut is painted with a large square, the *cauk* or *chowk*, representing the home of the goddess.

Such paintings in rice paste are profound and dramatic to behold, especially in contrast to the sombre atmosphere of the dwelling, for the Warlis live in square windowless huts made of wood, straw and mud. On entering such a hut the elemental simplicity of their lives is apparent; as the eye adjusts to the gloom, the majesty of their artistry in paint is revealed.

The first attentions of the academics in the 1970s were followed by the encouragement of India's Handicrafts and Handlooms Board. By providing brown paper and white paint a marketable commodity was created, producing not only a new source of income but also freedom from the ceaseless cycle of *cauk* painting. The folk art traditions of the Warlis are encapsulated in these extraordinary paintings – images that depict their everyday life, show epic legends, share local incidents and educate with

PAINTINGS OF THE WARLIS OF MAHARASHTRA

As with many of the mural painting traditions of India, the work of the Warlis transfers without any appreciable loss of creative energy and ingenuity to other media. These two details are taken from a painting on paper that depicts the tale of the magic bowl. Full of jungle lore, with depictions of tigers, trees, birds and ants, this story centres on a cautionary tale concerning the evil of wealth.

cautionary tales. The visual energy of Warli painting is now recognised around the world, with individual artists being singled out for special acclaim. Thanks to their humble and reserved outlook on life, the communities seem on balance to have gained from their exposure to Western civilization: the much needed income has not been accompanied by a destructive intrusion into their culture.

Another powerful school of wall painting, that of the women of Kumaon in Uttar Pradesh and Mithila in Bihar, belongs to a post-Aryan tradition. For the women of Kumaon the rites of passage and religious festivals provide the inspiration for *jyonti* and *patta* pictograms. The former shows three female deities, the consorts of the elephant god Ganesh; the latter is devoted to a particular deity of the seasonal festivals, such as Lakshmi at Diwali and Durga at Dussehra.

More dynamic in content and style, however, is the work of the women of the Mithila area in the Darbhanga district of Bihar. Centred on the market town of Madhubani, 'the forest of honey', the once domestic Mithila tradition of painting a colourful cornucopia of symbols and images on the walls and external verandah of the nuptial chamber, as well as within the room of the household god, is now regarded as a significant art form. Scenes from the Ramayana have always been favourite topics for these paintings, as well as representations of the deities, everyday village scenes, and auspicious symbols intended to confer fertility on a newly married couple. The energy, expressive power and sensitive use of intense colours has ensured great popularity for the Madhubani school of painting.

PAINTINGS OF THE MITHILA REGION OF BIHAR

The creative skills of the craftsmen and women of the lands around the settlement of Madhubani in north Bihar are renowned. For the peoples of Mithila, the rigours of life have proved no barrier, and indeed may have encouraged the establishment of a glorious tradition of wall painting. This area of flat alluvial plains, sandwiched between the foothills of the Himalayas to the north and the broad river Ganges to the south, is less well developed than many other regions of India, and densely populated. The rural peoples suffer from year to year the vagaries of the monsoon, and there is little or no surplus from a good harvest of rice.

Unlike the Warli tribal work, the Mithila paintings are part of an outstandingly fruitful folk art tradition. Both Warli and Mithila paintings became collectors' items some twenty years ago, but this has had little effect on the originality of their work, save to engender imitations.

Wall paintings originally came about as a response to the numerous cycles of rituals and vows, of which the thread-tying ceremony, when the higher caste boys are initiated into adulthood, and the celebration of a marriage, are pre-eminent. Auspicious images are painted in a style that is colourful and expressive rather than representational.

Seeking to improve the lot of these painters and their families, the government as well as visiting academics and collectors have fostered a wide range of alternative media suitable for creative expression. Without any lapse of energy this brightly coloured imagery has been transferred onto paper as cards, pictures and panels as well as onto plain cloth for cushions, scarves, shawls and saris. These examples of poster paint and pen work are typical of the prolific output of these artists, the rewards for which have provided a vital injection of income. The excitingly expressive spiralling image (far left) depicts Nagini, the snake goddess, who is lovingly depicted so as to appease so fearful a form. More recognisable is the image of the son of Shiva, Karthikeya, the god of war, decorated with an abundance of floral tributes (left).

THE PAINTER OF TEXTILES

The creative imagination, and evocative and educative power of India's wall painting tradition have also been applied since ancient times to the narrative scrolls, or *chitrakatha*, of the wandering bards. A popular medium of religious instruction, such entertainment must have thrived during the dark ages of the Hindu religion under Buddhist or Muslim empires. Today the bards continue to delight villagers with the myths and legends of the scriptures and tales of folk heroes. For the villagers of Rajasthan, imbued for more than 500 years with the spirit of martial heroism so beloved by their Rajput rulers, the tales of the bards, known here as *bhopas*, bring to life the epic battles and good deeds of local heroes such as Pabuji Rathore, and stories of the popular neo-Hindu deity, Dev Narayan. The legends are painted on long rectangular cloths, known as *phad*, some five metres by one and a half metres, by the Joshi clan of the *chippa* textile printing community. The cotton is sized and smoothed and the scenes of the adventure are outlined, then coloured with gum-based gouache. Finally the artist paints the eyes of the hero and life is breathed into the cloth. Rolled on two shafts of bamboo, the *phad* is carried from village to village, to be used as a backdrop for a night-time recitation of Pabuji's heroic deeds, which are recounted by the *bhopa* and his wife, accompanied by lively music and energetic dancing.

The painting of cloths for religious observance continues to inspire the artists and craftsmen of two communities in north-west India. Amid the urban clamour of Ahmedabad crudely executed shrine cloths powerfully serve the religious needs of the lowest castes of that industrial city. In contrast, the Brahman painters of Nathdwara in southern Rajasthan continue their calm devotion to the daily and seasonal needs of Krishna. The temples of this cult, more akin to rambling homes, provide every luxury for the comfort of the god, here known as Srinathji, including painted cloth backdrops to beautify the shrine and enhance the reverence of devotees. Known as *pichvai*, literally 'something at the back', they depict events in the god's life and are frequently changed as the cycle progresses. They are still executed by the specialist Brahman painters of this thriving town. The gentle Nathdwara artists are masters of detail, creating large hangings almost like a patchwork collection of miniatures. Commissioned by the temples of the sect from all over the world, their bright *pichvais* are now also popular as decorative hangings.

More dynamic are the expressive red and black cloth paintings known as *mata no chandarvo* and *mata ni pachedi*, that is, shrine canopies and cloth panels, a speciality of the Vaghri community

Originally paint was a medium exclusive to the walls of homes, the surfaces of which were prepared with a coating of clay, cow dung and lime paste, rubbed smooth. Paints made from lamp black and local seeds are applied to the wall with a frayed twig. Watching a scene unfold on the wall of a house is a magical experience; the hand darts from the pot to the wall, outlining the image with a sure, steady movement.

On a grander scale is the largely historic practice of using wall painting as a vehicle for tales from the religious epics, folklore and local history. The temples, palaces and mansions of such states as Kerala, Karnataka, Tamil Nadu, Andhra Pradesh, Orissa, Maharashtra, Gujarat, Rajasthan and Ladakh contain a wealth of murals depicting mythological scenes, royal occasions such as hunting parties and processions, and a host of folkloric tales. For the visitor to India the most accessible, prolific and exciting wall paintings are to be found in the princely state of Rajasthan. In a mural tradition that may date back to the eighth century, the forts, the *havelis* or merchants' mansions, and the rulers' palaces have been ornamented with all manner of artistry, often combining painted scenes with gilding, mirrors, semi-precious stones and marble inlay.

CLOTH PAINTERS OF RAJASTHAN

For many Hindu villagers, the tales of classical epics have been bolstered by colourful local stories. In Rajasthan such folklore is brought to life through the theatre of the wandering bards, known as bhopas, who tell of the epic battles and good deeds of local heroes like Pabuji Rathore. Such narration is brought to life by the unravelling of a phad, a colourful painted backdrop that serves as a pictorial reference for the narrator and audience alike (left). In the southern temple town of Nathdwara, by contrast, the shrine cloths (opposite) depicting Krishna as Srinathji are intended to impart a sense of aesthetic appreciation and reverence in the onlooker.

PAINTERS OF CLOTH

The cloths from Kalahasti in Andhra Pradesh are decorated freehand with a kalam pen. First, the cloth is spread out on the ground or a low wooden bench. The artist then sketches in charcoal the outlines of the figures and designs which may be of a non-traditional nature, such as scenes from the Bible or corporate logos, or may be taken from the Hindu epics as illustrated on early cloths (above) or cartoons. The kalam for fine line work is a pointed bamboo stick swaddled at the point with felt or wool that is tied to the cane by a net of string. This pad holds the dyestuff that is released down the point of the kalam and onto the mordanted cloth by slight variations of finger pressure. Black outlines are painted using a solution of salts of iron (right). The final colours of yellow, blue and green are then added. The Vaghri community of Ahmedabad demonstrate a quite different tradition in cloth painting, using block-printing and crude kalam work (opposite).

PAINTED PICTURES ON WOOD, PAPER AND GLASS

The Mughal style of miniature painting on paper continues to flourish in Rajasthan and Uttar Pradesh, imitating with remarkable precision the masterpieces of the past (opposite). The Thanjavur school of painting owes its origins to the commissions of the 18th-century Maratha kings. These paintings are characterized by their primary colours and low relief gesso, embellished with gold leaf and semi-precious stones. The portrayal of Balakrishna, the infant god, remains popular (left). The Thanjavur style of painting on glass is also in vogue and again images of Krishna are common (below).

METALWORK

**BLACKSMITH'S WARES
TO BRONZE IMAGES**

*In Gujarat, Rajasthan and
Madhya Pradesh, itinerant
blacksmiths are a common
sight. As makers and repairers of
domestic utensils and farmers'
tools, their work is indispensable
(left). The fine bronze (above) of
a south Indian master craftsman,
will, by contrast, be exported or
sold in a gallery.*

The metalworker of India continues to follow a tradition of useful, decorative and spiritually rich creativity that has a long and illustrious history, whether crouched over a burnished bronze icon shaded by the palm trees of the south; adding the final touches to the face with the delicacy of a surgeon; energetically pounding a rod of iron beside his cart in a dusty village street in the Thar desert; or brazing together the components of a brass temple vessel over an open fire in a back street of Benares.

The first true practitioners of physical science, metalworkers were accorded a high status in antiquity as the makers of robust ploughshares for the farmers and effective weapons for warriors. Their place in the caste system was established by vocation, separating the craftsmen into such classes as blacksmiths, domestic utensil makers and creators of icons. These guild and caste divisions among metalworkers are still evident today in village and city, from the rural blacksmiths and tribal metalworkers who serve the daily needs of the agricultural community to the urban metalworkers who produce an extraordinary variety of goods whether votive, decorative or utilitarian for a local, national and international market.

MAKERS OF UTILITARIAN METAL WARES

It is within the noisy back streets of the towns and cities of India that copper, brass and tin utensils are made. Carried to the surrounding villages by bicycle or bus-borne merchants, or haggled over at the bazaar shop by the wives on a visit to the local market, these metal wares are made to traditional shapes that combine beauty with robust utility.

As early as 2500 BC the technology of metalworking was already well developed as can be seen from the use of bronze, an alloy of copper and tin, in the casting of beautiful and technically admirable figures. From literary writings, especially the Rig Veda (*c.* 1000 BC), it is clear that copper- and bronze-working had reached the level of a specialised science, and the craftsmen involved were highly respected members of society. From such sources and from archaeological evidence, it is now known that the art of bronze-casting has been a continuous practice in the region for more than 5000 years. The working of iron also reached an impressive level at an early date. At the Qatab Minar mosque near Delhi stands a famous solid iron pillar, 7.2 metres tall and with a considerable length extending underground, which dates from about AD 400. The European iron industry did not attain the capacity to make such large castings until the nineteenth century. Moreover, the pillar is completely resistant to rust, and the capital and inscription remain sharp showing no signs of wear – a fact which modern metallurgists still cannot explain.

Parallel with these technical advances there developed a complex system of using various metals in religious observance, while they were also credited with beneficent and health-giving properties. As a means of ensuring longevity for the images of divine immortality, figures in a metal such as gold, silver, copper or bronze are preferred to their counterparts in stone and wood. In southern India, home to the great Hindu temple complexes, icons of bronze are believed to hold and radiate the energy of the divine. Certain metals are credited with alchemical and healing properties, as described in the Ayurvedic scriptures of medicine. Used in everyday life for cooking, as well as for the collection and storage of water, brass and copper are thought to have health-giving qualities.

THE BLACKSMITH

The blacksmith or *lohar* community of India extends from colourfully dressed itinerant families to settled groups in the towns and larger villages who forge everyday inexpensive utensils and implements. No home would be without their round iron skillets or *tawa* for the cooking of unleavened bread, the larger cooking vessels known as *karhai* and *patila*, a stove or *choolah*, and scissors, knives, vegetable cutters, ladles and spatulas. In contrast to the noise and bustle of the town and city workshops of the ironworkers' quarter, the rural blacksmith enjoys a peaceful and simple life, linked to the rhythms of the agricultural community. Such a blacksmith is often itinerant, for his metalware is long-lasting and he can only earn a living by supplying several villages. The names of these wandering ironworkers are various: perhaps the best known are the nomadic *gadia* (cart) *lohars* of the northern state of Rajasthan. The *malwias* are of a similar kind and are found throughout Madhya Pradesh; they are famed, unusually, for their fine workmanship in both iron and wood.

These footloose smiths and their families are a memorable sight: sitting in the shade of their bullock cart at the side of a village street or on a highway verge at the edge of a town. The wife of the *lohar* is more often than not found squatting impassively, cranking a hand-operated fan or bellows which raises the small pile of charcoal to an intense heat, as her husband beats out a ploughshare or hammers a spike from iron wire on a small anvil. It is to these blacksmiths that the villager will bring worn cooking pots, libation and water vessels for patching or tinning, while the farmer will order nails, hoe irons, axe heads and knife blades.

In Ladakh there is a comparable group of blacksmiths who also rely on the door-to-door merchandizing of their skills and wares. Known as *gara*, these craftsmen possess a range of metalworking skills that are central to the life of the people of the mountains. To save metal, a precious commodity in so remote a region, the *gara* devotes a large proportion of his working life to salvaging scrap as well as repairing old utensils. More creative is his manufacture and fitting of the large iron household stove, the *thap chabrik*, which is the proudly owned and essential centrepiece of every Ladakhi kitchen. Decorated with polished brass plates cut into designs of dragons, floral friezes, interlocking geometric compositions and propitious diagrams, these stoves are further ornamented with a colourful inlay of semi-precious stones. Other work includes the forging of splendid locks with complex multi-lever mechanisms. For these the design of the keys is no less inspired, and they form ornaments in themselves as they hang from the waist of many a householder.

The range of household wares produced by these craftsmen is extraordinarily diverse. Seen here (opposite) are the simple, undecorated and therefore inexpensive base metal food trays made in Jodhpur, Rajasthan, that are in contrast to the fine brass water pot production (above) in Udaipur, Rajasthan.

Travelling with their home and workshop packed onto a single cart, these itinerant blacksmiths (left), found in Barmer, Rajasthan, work as a family to produce simple ironwork for a wide-ranging clientele. Here, the wife of the hammer-wielding smith fans the charcoal embers of the tiny furnace.

THE TRIBAL METALWORKER

In India there are two very different groups of metalworkers who make great quantities of cast icons. The high-caste members of the *kammalan* community in the south work to the dictates of the Hindu scriptures. In contrast, the tribal artisans of the central and eastern lands create with expressive spontaneity. Such tribal peoples are scattered across the forests of less well travelled districts of central and eastern India: the western lands of West Bengal, southern Bihar, western Orissa and south-eastern Madhya Pradesh. The tribal artefacts, known loosely as *dhokra* work, are predominantly hollow-cast and are produced by the lost wax process, which has long been known to these pre-Aryan communities. It is by the free and rapid way in which they construct a model, unlike the fastidious wax work of their more elevated counterparts to the south, that the tribal metalworkers are able to achieve their exciting castings. In 1909, in his book *Castes and Tribes of India*, Edgar Thurston noted this characteristic in his description of the work of the Kuttia Kondh tribe of Ganjam and Koraput districts of Orissa:

The core of the figure is roughly shaped in clay, according to the usual practice, but, instead of laying on the wax in an even thickness, thin wax threads are first made, and arranged over the core so as to form a network, or placed in parallel lines or diagonally, according as the form of the figure or fancy of the workman dictates. The head, arms, and feet are modelled in the ordinary way. The wax threads are made by means of a bamboo tube, into the end of which a movable brass plate is fitted. The wax, being made sufficiently soft by heat, is pressed through the perforation at the end of the tube, and comes out in the form of long threads, which must be used by the workmen before they become hard and brittle.

By practised control of the application of these beeswax threads the craftsman can fashion the character of his model, whether the aim is finesse or crude expressiveness. For a god he may seek to show the divine intensity of the gaze, the fine folds in the clothing, the jewellery. In contrast, for a fanciful model of a tiger he will wrap a lattice of threads across the whole body to pattern it, and detail the head with a toothy smile. For further patterning or to rework sections of the model, a hot knife is used to smooth the surface, and wax strands are laid on again.

On the satisfactory completion of the solid wax or wax-coated clay model, a sheath of clay paste is carefully pressed all over

DECORATED IRONWORK FROM BASTAR

The blacksmiths from southern Madhya Pradesh forge and hammer iron into a most delightful range of oil lamps, tools and statues that depict animals, birds and men for their predominantly tribal clients. Using only a few tools and a simple furnace of a handful of coals, the smiths twist and bend the hot iron into expressive shapes. Such work is now appreciated by a wider audience.

it. This is the clay mould that will give the likeness of the wax model to the metal. For protection and strength, the layer of fine clay is then sealed with a wall of clay mixed with rice husks, which will burn away and leave holes that allow the casting to cool evenly. A channel is formed for the exit of the wax and the receipt of the molten metal. When the clay is dry the assembly is securely bound with metal wire. In order to release the wax, which is saved for re-use, and to prepare the clay for the intense heat generated by the molten metal, the wire-bound mould is grilled over the charcoal of the furnace. Then, from a small crucible, the molten metal is poured into the mould and allowed to set. For models with a clay centre the beeswax is not melted out; here, the pouring of the white-hot metal into the clay mould incinerates the wax and allows the metal to completely surround the core. The core may later be scraped out through a hole in the bottom of the casting, or alternatively it may be left to act as a weight, which lends additional stability to the casting.

To release the casting from the mould, the binding wires are cut away and the clay enclosure broken open with chisel and hammer. Any subsequent work, such as chiselling, scraping, filing and polishing, needed to complete the figure, depends on the finesse of the wax moulding, the success of the casting process and the desired character of the object. The free and varied techniques used to produce the wax moulds create an equally exciting diversity in the finished metal forms. Whether the work is naturalistic or stylized, a lively interpretation of a mythical creature or a filigree-adorned goddess of great beauty, it will have a tremendous freshness and strength which, on first discovery, sweeps across the senses. It is not surprising, therefore, that this provocative and charming tribal work is now sought after by foreign buyers. However, the regrettable result is that less lively imitations and dull copies are now widely on sale.

DOMESTIC METALWORK

Each region of India has its own range of cooking utensils that is intrinsically linked to diet. In the south, a land where vegetarians predominate, the cooking of rice and vegetables and the feeding of the many in the great temple complexes has produced platter-like cooking and serving vessels. Smaller pans, such as this example in a roadside eatery in Kerala (opposite), are known as uruli, their larger variants (below) from the temple kitchens as varpu. In complete contrast is a kitchen in the Himalayas, where the freezing winters of Ladakh are made tolerable by a central stove, decorated with auspicious designs (right).

THE MAKER OF USEFUL METAL WARES

Whether secure in a town *haveli* or sharing a mud-walled village house, the families of India share a need for the work of the town and city metalworkers. Set up in the back alleys of every large settlement in India, these workshops may be traced by the din they create. Here the craftsman forges, beats, cuts, rivets and burnishes the myriad of metal vessels and implements of ancient and traditional form that have changed but little over the centuries, matching perfectly the simple and equally unchanging needs of the Indian householder. Some of these undecorated metal wares are of unrivalled elegance. However, more modern plastics and mass-produced stainless steel goods are now tending to take the place of these traditional hand-wrought metal wares.

The most common metals in use, aside from the recent introduction of stainless steel, are brass and copper. The technology of brass production was known some 2000 years ago when this alloy, with an outward appearance of gold, was first discovered. In popular use since the third century BC, brass is made by fusing copper with zinc. Like copper, it improves in strength from repeated hammering during the shaping of the sheet metal into the desired form.

Water vessels, buckets and bowls are composed of a number of components cut from sheet metal. For a curvaceous water pot, or *ghara*, the sheet brass will be heated and hammered into the shapes of the three principle elements: the neck, waist and semi-concave base. Depending upon the form of the final object, malleable sheet metal can be hand-shaped by one of several processes with a hammer or mallet. Low, shallow forms are obtained by hollowing or sinking, in which a metal disc is hammered from the inside using a depression carved in a wooden block. Deeper forms can be raised. Such vessels are worked externally, starting at the base and continuing towards the rim using a ball-shape or domed stake. The overlapping or folded joints are soldered together by brazing over an open fan-driven furnace, and are made all but invisible by the diligent processes of hand-grinding and burnishing.

For the majority of homes that do not have a mains supply, the twice-daily fetching of water, in the morning and before dusk, is a ritual made elegant by the graceful carriage and bright attire of the young girls and women of many a community. From the pump, pond or well the water for the whole family's needs is collected by the women in metal vessels fashioned according to the traditions of the caste or community. Most likely to be made of brass, these containers are known as *churru* or *kalas*, and may be bulbous and rounded, or straight-sided and narrow-necked. The use of a metal vessel for carrying water signifies a family of means by comparison with those who have to use clay pots. Once in the home, however, the water is generally transferred to a portly clay pot, known as a *ghara*, and placed in or on the *panniyaru*, a ledge or niche which then becomes a shrine for the life-giving liquid. These unglazed clay vessels serve to cool the contents as the water slowly seeps through the body of the container and evaporates.

The way of life for Indian families calls for a great range of other metal utensils. For the ritual and frequent cleansing of hands, as well as for the drinking of water, everyone will own a waisted beaker known as a *lota*. Traditionally made of brass, these personal pots are now most popularly made of polished stainless steel. Of a more auspicious character, there are also special types of *lota* made in two sections, of brass and copper, signifying the meeting of the two rivers sacred to Hindus, the silt-rich waters of the Ganges and the clear flow of the Jamuna.

In the large-scale manufacture of utilitarian metalware in northern India, the state of Uttar Pradesh is predominant, and the centre of production is undoubtedly the city of Moradabad. From here comes the majority of the hand-made or hand-finished brass, copper and stainless steel implements of traditional shapes that are needed by town and city householders. Such wares have now become highly prized by the villagers for dowry exchange; a walk through the metal bazaar of many a market town in the north-west of India during the marriage season is often an exciting experience. Surrounded by a noisy gaggle of senior matrons and younger married women, the metal merchant sits in his shop, impassive before the onslaught of haggling. Fingering the wares, the women, often from herding or shepherd communities, look confidently at one another, each proudly bejewelled with an abundance of archaic silver ornaments matched by their finest garb, secure in their role as holders of the family purse.

In the south of India, the shapes and uses of everyday metal wares are often markedly different. A diet founded on rice and vegetables, rather than wheat and meat, has led cooking vessels to evolve into large-bodied and narrow-necked forms for boiling, complemented by shallow round dishes for simmering. Such shapes are well suited to both lost wax and sand casting techniques, processes in which the southern craftsmen excel. Each utensil has a specific name and use: the large *kudam* is for carrying water from the well or pump and is shaped to rest against the hip; for the storage of water there are the capacious *gangaalam* and *andaa*, often with the blood-red tint of beaten copper. Rice is cooked in the narrow-necked *thavalai*, pulses in the wider-mouthed *chutti paanai*, and vegetables and sweet dishes in the shallow and platter-like *uruli*. Many of these cooking utensils are made of bell metal, an alloy of copper and tin, which combines a pleasing old-gold tint with a useful resistance to tarnishing.

Of the utilitarian metalworking communities of the south, the bell-metal craftsmen of Kerala are famous for their casting and turning of the *uruli* cooking and serving dishes. Made in Palghat district in the north of the state, these household wares are dwarfed by the similarly shaped but wagon-wheel sized *varpu*. Made in Alleppey district on the Malabar Coast using the lost wax process, they are often well over 1.2 metres in diameter. The clients for such magnificent and elegantly simple castings are predominantly the kitchens of the southern temple towns. Suspended over the fire, *varpus* provide the means to cook and serve food for the many thousands of pilgrim visitors who each day flock to the enormous communal dining rooms of the temples.

THE MAKER OF IDOLS AND LAMPS

Among the processes that have developed to elevate an object to the realm of the sacred, the method of manufacture of a metal deity is in itself a religious ritual. The role of such craftsmen in this tradition has, therefore, become interlinked with that of the priests and learned men. The elaborate treatise on bronze casting found in the Shilpashastra, with its edicts on art and architecture, is studiously followed. This and other holy scriptures prescribe not only the types of metals and techniques, the physical measurements and proportions for each figure, but also include verses, or *dhyana*, describing each form, its characteristics and its symbolism. And yet such strict rules do not restrict creativity, for in the lost wax method no two castings are ever alike, and the devotion, desires and skills of the individual artist may be expressed in each individual icon. The combination of ascetic

TEMPLE SOUVENIRS OF THE SOUTH

The roadway leading to the Venkateswara temple complex at Tirumalai in Andhra Pradesh is lined with trinket sellers. Solid cast effigies of favoured deities, produced in the local village workshops, are displayed to attract the pilgrims (below).

purity and technological expertise needed by the maker of icons is elegantly portrayed in this prayer from the Agni Purana, to be recited the night before work commences: 'O thou Lord of all the gods, teach me in dreams how to carry out all the work I have in my mind.'

The great majority of the makers of fine cast icons are to be found in the south of India, in centres such as Bangalore and Mysore in Karnataka, Palghat in Kerala, Tirupati in Andhra Pradesh, and especially in the state of Tamil Nadu. Here the numerous centres include Swamimalai, Tiruchirapalli, Madurai and Salem. Members of the *kammalan* community, these high-caste craftsmen trace their descent from the god of the arts, Viswarkarma, through the offspring of his third son, Tvastram, who worked in copper and brass. Encouraged over the centuries by successive empires, these *sthapatis* or traditional architect-sculptors have a brilliant history of detailed and delicate icon casting. Of the great periods of patronage, the Chola empire proved to be the most inspiring. From the tenth to the thirteenth

SAND-CAST METAL FORMS

In the village of Kumbakonam in Tamil Nadu is a thriving industry making sand-cast oil lamps, made of brass. These workshops are more akin to small engineering works as each section of the lamp is cast in a sand mould (left) and then threaded on a lathe for assembly. The popular standing lamps (above) are used in the household temple and often adorned with the hamsa, or mythical swan.

figures balance vigorous energy with serene calm, illustrating the sweet balance of creation with destruction.

Happily, it is from these great works that the icon makers of the present day draw much of their inspiration. Faithfully copying the masterpieces of the past, the craftsmen in bronze supply two wholly disparate markets. Of these, the traditional demand from the temple and the wealthy faithful has been wholly eclipsed by the desires of the relatively new and thriving art market. This national and international phenomenon demands not only the production of works recalling the masterpieces of the past, but also an 'antique' finish, achieved by chemical baths which create a patina and calculated distressing with chisel, file and coarse sanding. Whether such work is indicative of a lack of creative ingenuity or a surfeit of the same is a matter of opinion. Certainly the twentieth century has proved to be no new era in creative originality in this art; but at least the thriving industry has ensured a continuity of technical skill and an increase in the number of practitioners, laying the foundations for a possible renaissance in the future.

The casting and forging of oil lamps is a craft of the south that feeds a thriving national market. Serving both a religious and a secular need, the *deepam* or lamp has become the most popular memento of the temple tourists, rich and poor, who throng from all the states of India to the pilgrimage centres of the south throughout the year. Such lamps have long been held as sacred objects, combining in their output of light and heat the symbols of Agni, the god of fire, and Surya, the sun god.

Following the pattern of archaic forms in stone and shell, these metal lamps are, at their simplest, composed of a bowl-shaped reservoir for the oil and a spout to hold the wick. From this simple basis a myriad of lamp designs has evolved. These include the popular standing variety, the *kuthu-vilakku*, with a five-wicked lamp bowl perched on a slim column made stable by a heavy pedestal. Many-tiered lamps of this type are often used at weddings, creating a dazzling pyramid of flickering flames, highlighting the symbolic metal forms, such as the *hamsa* or mythical swan, that stand above each cluster of wicks.

For home or temple use, small hand-held votive lamps or *aarathi* have a carved handle in animal form. Often to be seen in the temple sanctuary of Tamil Nadu is the *deepalakshmi* lamp, comprising a female statue carrying in the cup of her hands the shallow bowl for oil and wick. Hanging lamps were originally intended to provide a source of light under an archway, and are ingeniously contrived to contain large quantities of oil and a self-supporting wick within the svelte body of a bird or animal. The chain itself is often an object of great beauty, whether ornamented with acrobatic ladies or a finely made series of plain links.

centuries exquisite copper icons were produced from comparatively coarse wax models, so that the art of finishing each casting by chasing assumed a greater role. Later, the use of an alloy of five metals, known as *panchaloha*, became popular, the copper, tin, lead, silver and gold representing the five elements of earth, air, ether, water and fire.

The figures cast in the era of the Cholas are often masterfully sublime representations of the deities. Unlike the coarse work of the preceeding Pallava epoch or the overdecorated style of the subsequent Vijayanagara and Nayak dynasties, these icons are elegant, almost austere, showing a combination of grace in movement, sweetness in expression and simplicity in adornment. For many of the Chola craftsmen the summit of their creative genius is seen in an execution of the figure of Nataraja, the form of Shiva as Lord of the Dance. Dancing in the joy of knowledge and celebrating the destruction of evil within a halo of fire, such

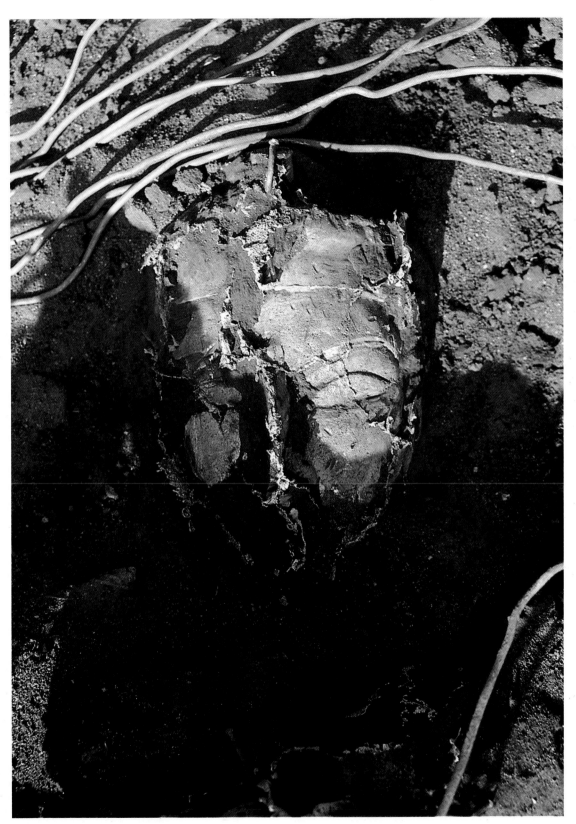

LOST WAX METAL CASTING

To achieve a detailed finish it is important to create as perfect a wax model as possible (opposite). Onto this form is pressed a coat of fine clay to create the mould, followed by a jacket of clay mixed with rice husks, made in two parts. The assembly is then bound by wire, ready for the pouring of the molten lead.

FROM FURNACE TO FINISHED FORM

A commission from the state government, this life-sized sculpture of Nataraja, Lord of the Dance, is being made by the lost wax process (left). Exhumed from the furnace pit, the face and body remain bound by the protective mould of clay and wire. After months of chiselling, filing and polishing, the effigy will be as detailed and lively as this hanging lamp (above).

THE LOST WAX CASTING PROCESS

For these makers of imitation Chola bronze images, cast by the lost wax process, the demands from abroad and the luxury market at home ensure an abundance of work. A master craftsman in Swamimalai employs a troupe of apprentices to work at each of the many stages of production. This goddess figure (above) has been freshly broken from its clay mould and is now ready to have the residual metal carbuncles removed. Using a sharp edged metal scraper, the bright metal contours of the body and garment folds of this effigy are slowly revealed (above right) and as with many a representation of a Hindu idol, the face or the eyes remain untouched until the last so as not to disturb its slumber prematurely.

After the initial scraping away of the surplus metal the craftsman wedges the sculpture between his bare feet, or against an upright, and proceeds to carve the details by using a range of finely honed chisels and a hammer, working from broad to narrow blades. The folds in the dress of this goddess (*opposite below*) are cut away with such a combination of tools.

As many as six or seven assistants will work in a studio at any one time, ensuring a constant production of finished effigies. After the final shaving away with the finest blades, the facial features are delineated, thus giving of life to the figure. Hours of polishing with various grades of coarse and fine emery cloth achieve a sparkling finish, seen here in the beatific representation of Saraswati (*right*). Many of the sculptures will be antiqued with a dull green patina to replicate more closely their Chola forebears.

JEWELLERY AND DECORATED METALWORK

A DELIGHT IN ADORNMENT

Dressed in her best beaded and embroidered finery, and laden with dowry jewellery, this young Rabari shepherd girl from Kutch in Gujarat (left) visits the local market town with her family. The men of the region are less well caparisoned and display their status by the wearing of a turban, earrings (above) and, sometimes, a silver choker.

The freedom with which so many of the men, women and children of India ornament themselves with all manner of jewellery reveals a deep-rooted love of adornment which transcends mere decoration and vanity. Indeed, the role of jewellery satisfies many needs. As well as the beautification of the body it has also had a further, historical function: that of acting as a store of portable and accessible wealth, a significant benefit in a land so prone to invasion from all quarters. While many cultures in other parts of the world have forgotten such associations, the peoples of the Indian subcontinent continue to be supported and enlivened by their faith in the talisman and the magical power of jewels and precious metals. The continuity of jewellery-making traditions is remarkable. Ornaments of all kinds, whether of common materials such as grass necklaces, thread bracelets and beaded fancies, or wrought in silver and gold with precious jewels, seem to have altered very little in form over the millennia. Not only have the shapes and uses of the rings, hair decorations, chokers and the like remained constant, but the design of their components remains remarkably unchanged, as can be seen in early examples, and sources such as sculptures, mural paintings and miniatures.

A PROFUSION OF HOLY BEADS

In their simplicity of materials and construction, and their widespread use as both ornament and talisman, the wooden bead necklaces of India maintain a link with the less sophisticated pagan cultures of the past. According to Hindu religion, certain trees are regarded as sacred and each god and goddess of the pantheon is assigned to a particular tree or bush. A boon would thus be granted to the makers and vendors of wooden beads, who are to be found in the vicinity of the many holy sites and temples of India. For the worshippers of Vishnu, for instance, the wood of the tulsi tree, known as the sacred basil, is cut, turned smooth and pierced for stringing as a necklace of small thin tubular beads (right). In the lands around Vrindaban and Mathura in Uttar Pradesh, the sites of the early life of Krishna, there is a thriving industry of tulsi bead-making (above left). For professional ascetics and the wandering holy men found throughout India, and especially in the vicinity of a holy site, the wearing of a profusion of prayer-bead necklaces is commonplace (below left). The dark red-brown knobbly berries from the rudraksha tree (Elaeocarpus ganitrus), which is dedicated to Shiva, are ever popular.

THE MAKER OF SIMPLE ORNAMENTS

The simple wooden ornaments of India retain a close association with the unsophisticated cultures of antiquity. They also retain their ancient magical role, providing adornment for the many temporary and professional ascetics found in the vicinity of a holy site. Much of this jewellery, as well as that of the tribal peoples, is a continuation of the primitive strings of pierced seeds, dried fruit and pieces of hollow plant stem that have been worn since the earliest times. Protective qualities are attributed to the various wooden bead trappings on sale in their hundreds of thousands at major temples throughout the land, such as the prayer bead necklace, strung with the dark red-brown knobbly berries from the *rudraksha* tree (*Elaeocarpus ganitrus*). The Vaishnavas use rosaries turned from the stems of the sacred basil or *tulsi* (*Ocimum sanctum*), while a vast number of Indians treasure a necklace of scented sandalwood as an aromatic souvenir of a fulfilling pilgrimage. The makers of holy wooden beads are frequently seen plying their trade near the temple; the craftsmen squat for hours, turning their hand lathes with a bow to shape the popular trinkets. To one side, with a seemingly nonchalant air, sits the satisfied shopkeeper and owner of the craftsman's labour, appraising the milling throng that flocks past.

In the villages and nomadic camps of many a district of central and north-western India, the tribal peoples and pastoralists have a great fondness for ornaments strung onto colourful thread or stitched into woven bands of yarn. It is not uncommon, for instance, to find a choker, made with a finely worked boss of silver from the local silversmith, sewn on to a simple knitted band of thread and secured at the back by a large, brightly coloured plastic button and loop. A simpler and equally elegant neck ornament is made by interlacing cotton or rayon yarn into a decorative band, sometimes enlivened by strands of metallic thread, beads or the ever useful buttons, as well as a scattering of base metal or silver hangings in the form of small bells, domestic gods or lucky mango leaves. The nomadic herding communities of the desert lands of Kutch in western Gujarat are especially fond of such accessories. Strings and braids of coloured cotton also have a symbolic function in India that cuts across all boundaries of caste. At the summer festival of Raksha Bandhan, it is the custom for a sister of any age to pay loving respect to her brother by tying a cord of cotton around his wrist.

In Ladakh, a unique festival headdress, known as the *perak*, continues to be worn by the women of the region. This hood-like leather attire encircles the forehead, rises over the crown of the head and falls down the back to waist level, and is decorated all over with turquoise, ruby and coral stones. The lizard-, snake- or fish-like profile that such a headdress suggests is reflective of the belief that women originated in an underworld inhabited by reptiles and aquatic animals. On their wrists the women wear conch shell bangles, or *tunglag*, which are knocked together in greeting. The craft of shell and glass bangle-making has a long history in the lowlands as well, and such ornaments are popular among women of all ages in the rural communities. Plain glass and plastic bangles in red or green are the mark of a married woman, and in the Gangetic states and to the southeast these will often be worn with a bright white circle of the magical conch shell.

Horn, ivory and white plastic are also turned to make circular wrist and arm decorations; such bangles are a typical mark of the married village women of the states of Gujarat and Rajasthan, who have settled at the home of their husband. Their plain ornaments of ivory are often tinted with colour, which is achieved by boiling the bangles in a solution of pigment, most commonly red; in time, this bright coating becomes worn and fades to a pleasing pink hue. Until the death of the husband, when such adornment is usually dispensed with altogether, these simple arm and wrist decorations are renewed as necessary, and especially at festival time. The making of conch-shell artefacts and ornaments was once a significant craft tradition throughout India. Now, however, it is a minor craft devoted mainly to bangles and the engraved and polished *shankh*, the horn of good omen used at temples, wedding ceremonies and festivals; Bengal remains the centre for their carving and preparation. Highly coloured and patterned bangles made of glass, plastic and shellac, on the other hand, are now fashionable trinkets, both for the domestic and the export market.

Despite the dramatic recent increase in their sale, the manufacture of bangles from shellac remains the business of the individual artisan or small workshop. The demands of the trade are small as it requires little equipment. At home, or on the steps of a shop, the craftsman gently heats a block of resin over a small charcoal brazier and rolls the ductile material into bangles of any size and thickness. In many of the towns of Rajasthan the shaping of inexpensive and highly coloured shellac bracelets is a common trade, particularly in Jaipur, where such bangles are often studded with glass gems and spirals of base-metal wire amid a wavy striping of other colours. Delhi is also well known for shellac work embellished with glittering foil and spangles, and imaginative styles of surface decoration are also to be found in the craft-rich districts around Madhubani and Muzaffarpur in Bihar. Amidst the villages of this area it is not uncommon to find

the bangle makers plying their trade from house to house. Once a commission is secured, the artisan will set up his brazier in the courtyard compound, and begin to make colourful trinkets for the women and children of each family.

Glass bangle production is carried out on a much larger scale. The Indian market is dominated by the produce of Ferozabad in Uttar Pradesh and Hyderabad in Andhra Pradesh. Many a street corner in cities, towns and villages all over India forms the pitch of a glass bangle salesman, appealing to the tastes of women of all ages with his racks of fluorescent, brightly coloured wares. Both centres make millions of hand-worked bangles each year. Ferozabad has gained a reputation for its plain colours and painted designs, while Hyderabad produces rather more exotic bangles, elaborately made with encrustations of metallic and multi-coloured glass beads.

BRACELETS AND BEADS

For many of the women of India bracelets signify their status in life. When worn the length of the arm, a young woman from a Rajasthani pastoral community (opposite) shows that she is married and lives with her husband's family. In Gujarat and Rajasthan, strings of glass and plastic beads provide adornment on dress panels (below) and the head pads for cushioning water pots (right).

SHELLAC BANGLES

Throughout northern and western India, the making of colourful bangles of shellac (above) is a popular occupation. The materials and tools required are few. First, a ball of shellac is heated to a pliable consistency over a tiny brazier, and then rolled into a tube. Strips of shellac in other colours can be wound onto the tube, the ends of which are then brought together and sealed by rolling (top).

LADAKHI HEADDRESSES

The luxurious fashions of a
royal family, and their
patronage, have helped to
establish a tradition in Ladakh
of sophisticated jewellery in gold
and silver, set with semi-precious
stones. The style is largely
Central Asian in character and
yet the most extraordinary
example of such adornment, the
perak headdress, is exclusive to
the region. Worn by the women,
this dramatic headwear comprises
a wide leather cobra-like hood
that extends from the forehead
over the hair and down beyond
the waist. Set with anything from
25 to 250 turquoise stones, this
magnificent attire is held, by its
association with the reptilian
dwellers of the underworld, to
possess powers of fertility. Its
origin remains obscure, but a
popular legend tells of how a
king took a wife from an adjacent
region where the wearing of such
a headdress was the custom and
thereafter the perak was adopted.

JEWELLERY OF THE FARMING COMMUNITIES

The regions of Rajasthan and Gujarat have proved to be a favourite destination for travellers to India. Here, more than in any other area, the tribes and communities continue to wear their strikingly individual attire of clothing and jewellery. The women, wearing their dowry jewels day and night as a precautionary habit, continue this custom, as witnessed in Kutch, Gujarat (above) and neighbouring Rajasthan (above left). Their menfolk (left) are not averse to wearing necklaces, earrings and chokers, often of solid silver or silver wire.

metals and jewels were embraced by the invading Aryans, and the associations of various objects and materials with certain gods made their wearing an act of worship in itself.

Amulets continue to provide reassurance, as shown in the wearing of rings on fingers and toes, necklaces, anklets, armlets, bracelets and chokers which are thought to protect these parts of the body. As was once the tradition in Europe, and still is in many Catholic countries, it is customary to offer small stamped base-metal images of ailing limbs and organs at temples in the hope of a cure. Many rural people wear from birth a silver image of a popular local deity on a string necklace. Indeed, almost any precious substance or form of ornament is allotted a protective role. Gold and silver worn against the flesh are held to be health-giving, especially when bathing. Each of the precious gemstones is thought to enhance or counteract the effect of a particular planet. For wholesale coverage one can wear the *nauratna* ring, or a similar necklace, set with nine stones representing the sun, moon and planets; care must be taken, however, that the gems are set in the correct order to have the desired effect.

For the Hindus jewellery also provides a symbolic mark for each phase in the cycle of life. Ears are pierced for earrings at an early age, childhood is symbolically ended by the wearing of the sacred thread across the torso as a symbol of entry into responsibility, and in southern India a necklace is given or tied at the marriage ceremony. After marriage the women proclaim their new status by their ornaments: in northern India, for example, they wear glass bangles and toe rings. The familiar wearing of large quantities of gold and silver jewellery by many of the married women of India has yet another protective role. Provided by her own family, such wealth is her birthright and guarantees financial independence in times of need, especially if she is widowed. Indeed, at the death of her husband, a widow is expected to shatter her bangles and put aside her jewellery. Finally, at the end of life, precious metal serves to deter evil and ensure purity: a piece of silver or gold leaf, wrapped in a holy basil leaf, is placed in the mouth of the corpse.

It is obvious from the Vedic and Puranic scriptures that from an early date the nobility wore and hoarded magnificent jewellery in precious metals as a mark of distinction. In the Mahabharata, in the description of the wager at Hastinapura, Yudhisthira is described as losing first a very beautiful pearl; next a bag containing a thousand pieces of gold; next a piece of gold so pure that it was as soft as wax; next a chariot set with jewels, and hung all around with golden bells; next 1000 war elephants with golden howdahs set with diamonds; next 100,000 slaves all dressed in good garments; next 100,000 beautiful slave girls, adorned from head to foot with golden ornaments . . .

THE GOLDSMITH AND SILVERSMITH

Ornaments found at sites where the Indus Valley civilization flourished show that by 2500 BC India already possessed advanced jewellery-making skills. Many pieces have the forms of natural objects. Copper hairpins and armlets have been found decorated with animal motifs, and ear and neck jewellery shaped like lemon and *pipal* (*Ficus religiosa*) leaves. Later, the ancient animist beliefs in the protective qualities of ornaments, precious

The material wealth of the élite also served as a form of supplication to temple deities, and such munificence helped to ensure that respect for royalty was associated and imbued with the qualities of divinity. Judging by the lavishness and brilliance of the gold and jewels that drape many of the important icons throughout southern India today, it is no wonder that the Afghans so often came over the mountains to raid the Hindu pilgrimage sites ten centuries ago.

After largely indigenous developments in the style of Indian jewellery, the domination of the Muslim empires throughout the north and centre of the land introduced fresh fashions and techniques. It is thought that nose jewellery owes its origin to these invaders, and certainly ornaments became more lavishly detailed under their suzerainty through such techniques as enamelling and the setting of stones in gold leaf, as well as through the sheer profusion of jewels. The figurative expression so beloved by the Hindus was enriched by the formal and geometric rigour of the Muslim style.

The jewellery of gold and gemstones worn by the nobility was mimicked by their subordinates, but an independent identity in ornamentation is also clearly evident. As the second ranking precious metal, silver has come to be associated with the jewellery of the lower classes. This view has resulted in a mode for ostentatious dowries in which gold ornaments are regarded as indispensable, but even before this development the demand for gold always exceeded the indigenous supply. It is no wonder, therefore, that the gold- and silversmiths have traditionally been associated with perfidious miserliness. Nevertheless, silver continues to be the happy preserve of the rural peoples, whose men and women are often seen bedecked in a wealth of this metal crafted into forms that are delightfully expressive.

Many of the tribal and nomadic pastoral peoples of India, men and women alike, are also laden with quantities of predominantly silver jewellery, which serves not only as ornament but as a means of identification, a mark of status and a guarantee of financial security, as it has done for many millennia. No less traditional is the display of gold by the nobility of the land, as portrayed in the Ramayana:

Sita is represented as arrayed for her marriage with Rama in a light sari-like garment of a rosy red colour embroidered with gold, and with jewelled butterflies and other bright ornaments in her raven-black hair. Her ears are resplendent with gems, she has bracelets and armlets on her arms and wrists, a golden zone binds her slender waist, and golden anklets her ankles. She has jewelled rings on her fingers, and golden bells on her toes, that tinkle as she walks with naked feet over the carpeted floor.

THE SILVERSMITH

In many states, traditional silver jewellery is of a high grade and acts as a form of portable currency, identity and prestige. The village silversmith creates all manner of trinkets from blocks of the precious metal with the most rudimentary tools. Using kerosene or vegetable oil as a fuel this Rajasthani silversmith (right) funnels his flame with a brass tube to join two pieces of silver with an alloy of the metal. First, the silver is melted down and beaten with a hammer into either a sheet, or a square rod which is then drawn into wire. Such sheet or wire is beaten over a die to form the components (far right below) of a linked piece of jewellery. A similar effect may be achieved by chasing, whereby a sheet of silver is set into a bed of shellac on a wooden board and the patterns created with a hammered punch.

Such a description of a bride would fit a modern wedding in a merchant family of Bombay or the royalty of an erstwhile princely state.

The silver- and goldsmiths have, therefore, enjoyed a splendid continuity of patronage over the centuries. Known, according to region, as the *sonar*, *agasala* or *panchallar* in the south this craftsman belongs to the select *kammalan* community, and is held to be a descendant of the fifth son of Viswarkarma, Visvajna, who was a gold- and silversmith and jeweller. Throughout India there is a preference for the use of particularly pure gold and silver in the best jewellery, such as the finely wrought pendants, earrings and bracelets fashioned for dowries. The craftsmen have at their disposal a wealth of techniques, such as shaping, engraving, punching, casting, enamelling, inlay, granulation and filigree with which to fashion baubles, bold or delicate, as commissioned by their clients.

And it is by way of commissions, rather than the purchase of ready-made goods, that the majority of valuable jewellery has

SILVER JEWELLERY

By means of die-stamping and chasing, the village silversmith is able to fashion a tremendous variety of precious jewellery for the women of the community as well as for the more footloose pastoralists of the district. As a result of centuries of trade between Gujarat and the Middle East, East and North Africa, there is a striking degree of commonality in design. Motifs and techniques often echo each other as can be seen in these earrings (right) and a chain decorated armlet (above right).

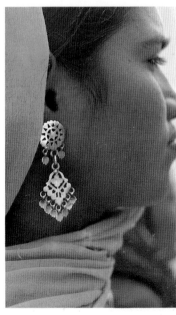

FINE GOLD AND ENAMEL JEWELLERY

The back streets of Benares are home to many a master jeweller. The art of enamelling and the open setting of stones is practised in the workshops of families whose pedigrees sometimes stretch back for four generations. Working at a low table (right) a craftsman sets precious stones in a bed of gold with nimble precision. Each article is reversible (above) so that both surfaces are equally beautiful.

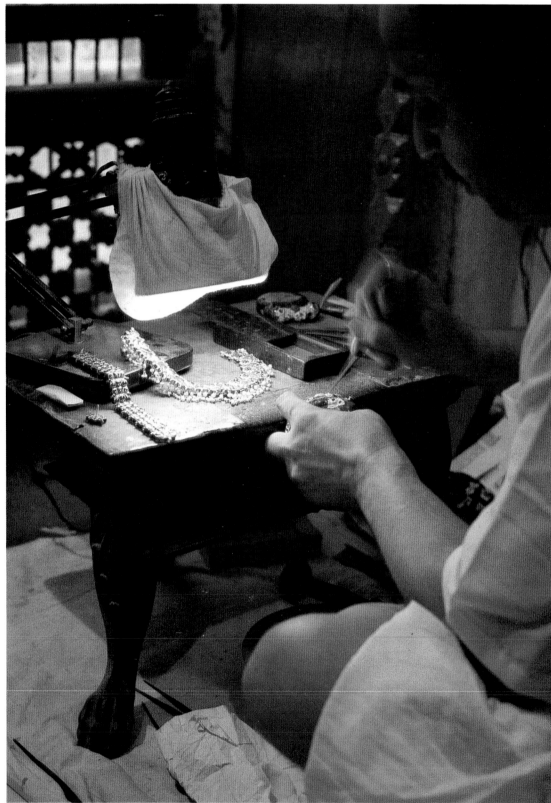

been made over the centuries. In the gold- and silversmiths' quarter of any town or city in India, as well as in many a village, it is all too easy to pass by the shop of the maker of these desirable ornaments without noticing it. Within a space often no larger than a single doorway, seated cross-legged before a large safe and beside a small glass cabinet, he works with a brazier, lamp, blowpipes and simple tools for cutting, paring and shaping. Such a paucity of tools and stock in hand should not be attributed to poverty: the craftsman is often selling only his labour, and the goods are owned by the merchant who deals with the client. Also, the manufacture of jewellery is often highly specialized, especially in towns. An ornament in the making might pass through the hands of three or more craftsmen, such as the engraver, or *chatera*; the setter of stones, the *kundansaz* or *jaria*; and the enameller, or *meenakar*. In the villages, on the other hand, the *sonar* must be the master of a variety of processes to meet the somewhat more elementary requirements, usually in silver, of his clients.

The silver trappings of tribal and village people, especially in the north and centre of India, are often most spectacular and more an extension of the body than an adornment. Developed out of a tradition that blends pre-Aryan, Mediterranean and Arab influences, as seen by the striking similarity of certain designs in all these regions, such silver jewellery is bulky yet finely detailed with stamped beaded wire and triangular granulation motifs. The women may be particularly well decorated with silver: on the forehead rests the spherical pendant or *tikka* echoed by, perhaps connected to, the dangling earrings known as *jhumkas*; around the neck, a collection of beaded and thread bands is crowned by what is often the most impressive ornament, worn at all times by men as well as women, the choker or *hansli*. The nose will invariably be pierced and may bear a small jewelled or silver stud, known as a *nathu*, or be laden with a weighty ring and disc of metal known as a *bhanvatiya*, linked by a chain to the adjacent ear. For the waist there is the *kandhani* or *taqri* girdle, and for the wrists and arms a series of wide bracelets, or *kada*; similarly, *kadi* embellish the ankles. Finally, the toes of married women are musically adorned by *chakti* rings.

The tribes and pastoral communities of Jammu and Kashmir, Himachal Pradesh, Rajasthan, Gujarat, Maharashtra and Madhya Pradesh delight in brightly patterned costume set with silver ornaments. Articles of particular value are reserved for the wedding display, but many of these embellishments are worn every day or when visiting the fairs and festivals beloved by these peoples. A more refined form of silver work is produced by the Orissan craftsmen of Cuttack. Here, fine silver threads are manipulated and soldered into place to form the filigree

decorations on a central and heavier wire frame. Popular motifs include roses, lotus flowers, butterflies, parrots and peacocks, all of which are used to decorate earrings, necklaces, brooches, hairpins and belts. Larger decorative metal forms such as rosewater sprinklers, bowls and model animals and birds are also made using this technique.

Most of the major cities of the north and south of India have their own individual stylistic traditions when manufacturing fine

REGIONAL VARIATIONS

Many an Indian town or city has a reputation for excellent workmanship in a regional style. Here, a craftsman of Udaipur assembles a delicate gold earring for a client's wedding trousseau (above). The elegantly studded gold bracelets (left) from south India are in contrasting style.

gold jewellery for the wealthier members of society. Delhi, Jaipur and Benares are renowned for their Mughal-inspired setting of stones, known as *kundan*, in which gems are bedded in a surround of gold leaf rather than secured by a rim or claw. Such sparkling and gleaming work, often seen as a costly necklace and matching earrings for a lucky bride, may be combined with *meenakari* enamelling. This is a *champlevé* technique: that is, a recess is hollowed out in the surface of gold or silver to take a mineral, such as cobalt oxide for blue, which is then fired into the depression so as to leave a thin gold line separating the segments of colour. The intricate designs echo and almost rival the jewels which they surround.

The gold jewellery of the south, particularly Andhra Pradesh, Tamil Nadu and Karnataka, has a distinguished pedigree. Jeweller, gold- and silversmith alike all follow the edicts of the scriptures when working on ornaments to clothe the figures of the gods, or when making finery for a bride. The bright gold and precious stones blend with the shape of the body in a most sensuous manner. Set on the head and running along the hairline and centre parting is the *thalaisaamaan*, a heavy and elaborate linked hair band that is studded with rubies, emeralds, uncut diamonds and pearl drops. Discs of gold and precious stones are laid on either side of the central crown; these are thought to invoke the health-giving brilliance of the sun and the peace, calm and romance of the moon. Equally elaborate are the hair decorations for the back of the head: these may include the *naagar*, a five-headed serpent in gold; or the circular *raakkadi* depicting a stone-encrusted swan. From a lotus-shaped stud decked in rubies or diamonds fall the *jimikki*, bell-shaped ear drops of gold and stones; often the whole piece is supported by a chain hooked into the hair above the ear. Piercing the nose on the right side there may be a gem-clad gold ornament in the shape of a swan, the *hamsa besari*; or at least there may be a jewelled *nathu*, placed through the left nostril. Around the neck dangles a gold chain

ENAMEL JEWELLERY FROM BENARES

The superior enamel work of Benares is also ravishingly successful in the round, such as on chokers and bracelets (right). These techniques, inspired by a mix of Muslim and indigenous styles, differ from those used in goldwork of the south, such as these bridal pendants (above).

supporting the marriage talisman, the *thaali* or *mangalasuthra*, shaped or patterned in a motif associated with the bride's community, often the lingam of Shiva or the conch and discus of Vishnu. Equally protective are the strings of pearls, reputed to ward off calamity, which support an amulet or pendant set with a pattern of stones. On the upper arm is set the inverted V-shaped *vanki* of either plain or gem-studded gold and, in a dance of light along the lower arms there is a rack of bangles, known as the *valai* or *kankanam*. To match the shape of the *vanki* there is a finger ring known as a *nali*, and around the waist is wrapped a tight-fitting stone-encrusted belt, the *oddiyaanam*, which is designed to maintain and highlight a desirably svelte figure. To show respect for the gods, the feet which touch the holy earth are covered with ornaments wrought of silver: anklets or *golusu*, in solid bands or chains, and heavy *metti* rings for the toes.

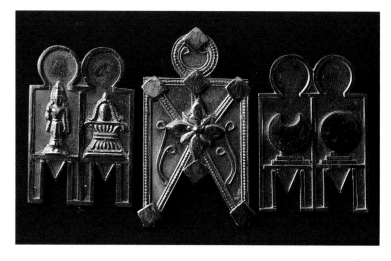

THE JEWELLERY OF A BRIDE

Until this century the only legal property a Hindu woman owned was her dowry jewellery and so, throughout every community in India, there has developed a tradition of investing in precious ornaments for the bride. This bride from West Bengal (above) wears all the finery that befits her status, including gold, silver and enamel work inlaid with precious stones, all given extra lustre by the fine silk and gold brocade sari from Benares.

The conspicuous display of jewellery has always been an important Indian tradition, strengthened by the rise in wealth of the majority. But costume jewellery and jewellery set with synthetic stones have also become popular, their production serviced by the stone grinders of towns such as Tiruchirapalli in Tamil Nadu (left).

THE MAKER OF DECORATED METAL WARES

The enhancement of everyday metalware by surface patterning and the creation of ornamental trinkets owes much to the craft of the gold- and silversmith and the jeweller, for they frequently share techniques and materials as well as clients. Metalware may be decorated with punch work, engraving, inlay and enamel; the last two techniques were introduced and refined by the Muslims, carrying the fashion from Persia, and reached a zenith of achievement under the patronage of the Mughal lords.

The metalworkers of the city of Moradabad in northern Uttar Pradesh, like many a decorator of metal throughout the subcontinent, flourished during Mughal rule, and they continue, by their efforts, to dominate the Indian market for engraved as well as utilitarian brass ware. Workers in sheet brass are known as *thatera* and those who cast the metal as *bharatias*. Although many of the processes are now semi-mechanized, engraving continues to be done by hand. Plates, ewers, bowls, boxes and coffee pots are engraved with a range of floral and geometric patterns, and these compositions are often inlaid with brightly coloured lac or vegetable resin. The decoration may include crudely worked scenes reminiscent of the style of Mughal painted miniatures, but often portray incidents from the Hindu scriptures.

Very much more specialized and refined in technique, style and patronage are methods which involve the use of precious metals and complicated sequences of inlay and enamelling. Of these processes *bidri* is the best known; it is named after the Deccan town of Bidar in north-eastern Karnataka. The process itself is thought to have been brought to India from Iraq many centuries ago, and involves the patterning of a blackened alloy of copper and zinc, often in combination with tin or lead, with a surface inlay of gold or silver wire or sheet. This form of decoration is often worked on rounded containers such as bowls, as well as caskets, and includes delightful combinations of fine lattice work interspersed with floral clusters, leaves and flowers. There are two principal techniques: the inlay of gold or silver wire, or *tarkashi*, and the inlay of precious metal sheets, known as *teh-nishan*. First, the ornament is wiped with a copper sulphate solution that temporarily blackens its surface prior to the sketching of the design with a sharp metal point. Enlarged by chasing with a chisel, these channels are filled with gold or silver wire or sheet, which is hammered into place. The surface is lightly abraded before being immersed in a solution of ammonium chloride and Bidar clay which permanently blackens the background. When burnished with oil the inlay is revealed.

Linking the craft of jewellery-making with that of decorated metalware are the artisans of the cities of Cuttack in Orissa and Benares in Uttar Pradesh. Their silver wire filigree work extends from small baubles to free-standing animal forms; in the latter the *meenakari* enamel technique is used to decorate howdah-clad elephants and proud peacocks, made in a variety of sizes suitable for mantelpiece ornaments. Silver and gold boxes are treated in the same way. The enamel ware of Benares is especially sought after for its soft pink hues, often combined with iridescent blue and green enamels. The *sergars* or silversmiths of Ladakh make a range of artefacts to fit the way of life of these Buddhist mountain dwellers. As well as making jewellery set with coral and turquoise, for which they are renowned, they also produce copper or brass cooking pots and sundry kitchen utensils. But their fame and wealth lie with their production of prayer wheels and tea kettles, fashioned from an amalgam of copper, silver and brass. The village of Chilling has been known for this craft for over 350 years, and its highly ornate tea kettles continue to be

made in traditional fashion, with a copper body and lid, and a handle and base of intricately decorated silver.

Still more elaborate is the famed *thewa* work of Pratapgarh, near Chittorgarh, in southern Rajasthan, which has been continously produced by four families of goldsmiths for the last four centuries. *Thewa* is a method of decorating red or green glass plates, panels, boxes, caskets and sundry ornaments with gold leaf. The gold leaf is embedded in a cake of shellac, which is then cut and punched with precision to create the requisite design or composition. The framed glass panel to be decorated is heated and the patterned gold leaf placed on its surface, to which it then bonds. The piece is heated further until the gold fuses on to the glass. For a dramatic effect, silver foil is placed beneath the glass to give a reflected glow. The effect resembles a miniature painting in gold, with scenes ranging from Rajput court life to Indian epics.

PRECIOUS METAL ORNAMENTS

Ladakh is well known for its fine precious-metal wares made by the silversmiths of the region. This statue of Buddha (opposite) is being adorned with precious stones and the silver collar (above left) will decorate the neck of a teapot. From Partabgarh in Rajasthan comes the delicate thewa goldwork (above) and from Bidar in Karnataka originate bidri wares (top).

THE SILVERSMITHS OF CHILLING

The pride of many a Ladakh household – the ornate butter teapots made of copper, silver and brass – are made by the silversmiths of Chilling (overleaf). The village has long been established as a centre for decorative metalwork; craftsmen spend many hours fashioning the simple shapes of prayer wheels, cooking vessels and teapots with the gentle tapping of a mallet.

TEXTILES

COLOURS AND PATTERNS OF INDIA

Cotton cloth has been India's foremost trading commodity since before Roman times. These reams of cloth (left) in Balotra, Rajasthan, will be screen printed for dress yardage; hand-blocked patterns (above) come from the same region.

From pre-Roman times to the present day, the dyeing and patterning of cloth has been the most desired of India's crafts. For the Mediterranean world in antiquity, the sheer muslins of the Gangetic delta were an exotic and expensive luxury. In contrast, some thousand years later, the cheap printed cottons of north-west India were to become an important international commodity, traded from the Mediterranean to the Indonesian archipelago, and Indian patterned fabrics later transformed European fashion and interior decoration with their clear, vivid colours. Happily, and despite the centuries of change wrought by the vagaries of the export market, this craft continues to form an integral part of the cultural heritage of the subcontinent. The extraordinary range of textiles available in India reflects in part the varying ability of different cultures to adapt established techniques and constantly changing styles to meet the current needs of the ever flourishing home and export markets. Now, in another upswing in the cycle of popularity, the skills of the weaver and dyer are in great demand again, whether from the fashion houses of Europe and America or from the visitor − for textiles are the most useful and portable, as well as the least costly, of all the crafts of India.

THE DYER

For many a new visitor it is the colours of India that provide a thrilling introduction to the culture of the land – not the colours of the landscape or the sky, but those seen in garments, turbans and hangings. As might be expected, this use of colour extends beyond outward appearance. In the words of Pupul Jayakar (*Marg*, xv, 4, 1962):

In India the sensitivity to colour has expressed itself in painting, poetry, music, and in the costumes worn both by peasant and emperor. Raga was the word used both for mood and dye. Colours were surcharged with nuances of mood and poetic association. Red was the colour evoked between lovers: a local Hindi couplet enumerates three tones of red, to evoke the three states of love; of these, *manjitha*, madder, was the fastest, for like the dye, it could never be washed away. Yellow was the colour of Vasanta, of spring, of young mango blossoms, of swarms of bees, of southern winds and the passionate cry of mating birds. *Nila*, indigo, was the colour of Krishna, who is likened to a rain-filled cloud. But there is another blue, *hari nila*, the colour of water in which the sky is reflected. *Gerua*, saffron, was the colour of the earth and of the yogi, the wandering minstrel, the seer and the poet who renounces the earth. These colours when worn by peasant or emperor were but a projection of the moods evoked by the changing seasons. The expression of mood through colour and dress was considered of such consequence that special colours were prescribed to be worn by a love-sick person and a person observing a vow.

Such spirited and inspired use of colours and their combinations have been well served by the proficiency and creativity of the dyeing communities who, until the late nineteenth century, worked exclusively with natural dyes. There are over 300 dye-yielding plants endemic to India which, when prepared with various mordants used in the appropriate quantity, create a myriad range of colours, tones and shades to delight the wearer and onlooker alike.

The technical challenge, from the first, was to fix colour on cotton. Unlike animal fibres such as silk, sheep's wool, or horse, goat or camel hair, vegetable fibres such as cotton will not accept most natural dyes as a permanent colouring. From an early date, therefore, practices were discovered, developed and adapted by which dyestuffs could be made to indissolubly coat or bind to the surface of the cotton fibres. In most cases this was achieved by the use of metal salts as intermediary substances between the cotton and the dye. Such a chemical 'bridge' is known as a mordant, a word derived from the Latin *mordere*, meaning to bite: the mordant 'bites' the fibre to lock the dyestuff to it, and so fixes the colour.

These natural dyes are either 'adjective' or 'substantive' by nature: that is, they either need a mordant or will bind by themselves. Although most vegetable dyes are of the first kind, there is an important exception. The leaves of the shrub *Indigofera tinctoria* yield a dark blue substantive dye, indigo. The strength and fastness of its colour led to a thriving trade in indigo between

THE ART OF DYEING

From Karnataka where the dyeing (above) and weaving of silk is pre-eminent, to Rajasthan where the dyeing of cotton with indigo and alazarin (opposite) is a long established craft, the colouring of cloth is ubiquitous throughout India.

THE COLOUR OF COTTON

India possessed an early knowledge of two crucial resources – cotton and fast dyestuffs. By 2500 BC there existed a demand for the dyeing and weaving of cotton fibres, processes not fully appreciated in Europe until the 17th century. It is rare not to find a riverbank carpeted with colourful cotton cloths, drying in the sun.

India and the West until the invention of synthetic dyes in the 1850s. Indigo is insoluble in water, so the leaves are treated with an alkali to make the substance temporarily soluble. On looking into the vat it seems not to have dyed the cloth at all. Only when the white fabric is pulled out and exposed to the air does the blue colour develop as the indigo oxidizes. A second dip may be given to darken the tone.

The necessary mordants for adjective dyes include metallic salts such as alum and compounds of chromium, iron and tin; salt; vinegar; caustic soda; slaked lime; urine; and substances prepared from leaves, fruits and wood ash. These are used singly or together. It is by the judicious mixing and sequence of use of mordant and dye, kept secret for generations, that the dyers

solution of the flowers of the myrobalan tree with bark from the mango tree, using an alum solution as a mordant. Always a difficult colour to create from natural substances, a semi-fast green tone is commonly obtained by overdyeing blue with the same myrobalan mixture.

After many millennia of use in the rituals of Indian life, it is no wonder that natural dyes have won a revered status, so that the introduction of synthetic substitutes in the late nineteenth century was said to have 'injured the artistic feelings of the people and demoralized the indigenous crafts'. Unfortunately, these chemical substitutes are simple to use on all types of yarn, are easy to transport and use and, most attractive of all, are cheap. The selecting and mixing of colours is now more straightforward and their supply, and therefore price, is no longer dependent on the vagaries of the monsoon climate. It is not surprising, therefore, that synthetic dyes now form the predominant colours in the textile industry of India. Where there is a gain in convenience from this technology, however, there is a loss of colour quality. Natural materials are not pure, and the pleasing hues of a red cloth dyed by the old method are due to this impurity, which gives a muted, slightly uneven colour. A red from a chemical source will, by comparison, be a stark pure colour, with no tonal movement or life to it. Happily, the tastes of the export market have led to a return to traditional methods in some of the dyeing communities, and the production of naturally dyed textiles has grown over the past two decades.

Whether of natural or synthetic origin, the dyestuffs of today are applied to cloth mostly by the *rangrez* community of workers – from the words *rang*, meaning colour, and *rez*, to pour. The indigo dyers have another title, that of *nilgar*, from *nila*, or indigo. Now, as in the past, all the dyeing communities are located near a reliable source of water, for the rinsing of cloth is as important as the dyeing itself. Some locations have particular advantages: at Jamnagar in Gujarat the water is held to give a particularly bright red hue to cloth, and at Masulipatnam in Andhra Pradesh the mineral-laden river waters transmit a particular clarity and sheen to textiles.

And so throughout India, especially in the north and north-west, colonies of dyers are to be found by the banks of the larger rivers, their sheds and the lengths of cloth set out to dry betraying their presence. Amid swathes of fabric blazing with the much loved strong colours of devotional orange, ocean blue, acid yellow and fresh green, the dyers ply their trade, guiding the cloth from the steaming dye baths through the hand-operated mangles. It is hard and repetitive work colouring plain fabric in quantity, and one sees no evidence of the alchemical mysteries that used to surround their trade.

of India have been able to create and fix the most difficult colours, of which the reds pose the greatest challenge. These shades, which are much in demand in India, are achieved by combining a source of the dyestuff alizarin, such as *chay* (madder), with alum, creating colours that can range from pink to deep red. Black is achieved by mixing an acidic solution of iron – often simply obtained from rusty scrap metal – with tannin from tree bark, or *jaggery* (palm sugar). Turmeric is an auspicious plant whose roots yield a strong yellow dye that is easy to use but not fast; such dyestuff is therefore used as a bright and sacred colour wash for the memorable turbans of the north-west of India, and as a top coat of dye to create mixed colours such as green. Yellow colouring of a more permanent nature is achieved by mixing a boiled

THE TIE-DYER

Beyond the world of the *rangrez* is the more elevated realm of the men and women who apply patterns to cloth. The festoons of brightly coloured and decorated yardage seen drying on the river banks and rooftops of western and central India are the craft work of both *chippa* and *khattri* communities, who do block printing as well as tie-dyeing. Found mainly in the old quarters of the towns and cities, these groups of artisans work intimately with each other to satisfy the orders of the merchant middlemen who, more often than not, supply and own all the raw materials for the work in hand.

Known with wry familiarity to many a textile design student and follower of 1970s fashion trends in the West, the technique of tie-dyeing in India takes an essentially simple process of colour patterning on cloth to the highest form of textile expression. Such textiles are known as *bandhani*, from the Sanskrit word meaning to tie, and their production is more often than not a co-operative effort between the men, who do the dyeing, and the women, who tie the cloth. For a simple pattern, a washed and bleached length of plain cloth is folded once or twice, and a pattern of dots is daubed in red on the top surface by the dyer. It is then passed on to the women, who pinch up the coloured parts of the cloth and tie them with wrapping thread, sometimes also applying a further 'resist', such as an impermeable coating to exclude dye. Back in the hands of the dyer, the cloth is immersed in the first and lightest of the dye baths, and then a further pattern is tied. The cloth is then given a second, darker dye bath; the process may be repeated again and again if further colour or a more complex pattern is needed. The finished cloth, with two or three bright colours against a dark background, is always sold with some of its ties still intact, showing that it is a genuine *bandhani* and not a cheap printed imitation.

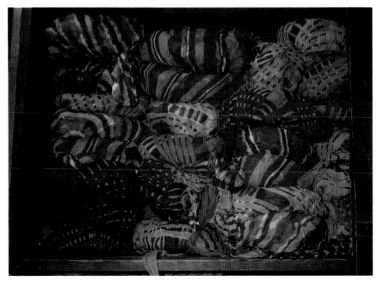

When the threads are removed and the cloth stretched out, the areas saved from the action of each dye will appear as different coloured circles, pinpricks, square patterns, rosettes and palmettes. The combinations and complexities of pattern and colour are endless; in general, the finer the cloth, and thus the smaller the areas of fabric that can be raised and tied, the more elaborate and refined the pattern that may be accomplished. Some silk examples are spattered with tiny dots of colour which combine to form a trellis of flowers, birds and foliage.

Simple-patterned *bandhani* textiles are inexpensive and allow the women of the poorer communities to dress in colourful regalia. When tied with many knots, however, the price of *bandhani* cloth rises steeply. Silk fabric with fine *bandhani* work is often worn as bridal attire by women of the richer merchant communities.

Bandhani work is particularly prized by the farming community of Rajasthan and Gujarat, whose women sport brightly coloured and spotted headcloths and shawls – *odhnis* and *dupatta* – while the men are resplendent in polka-dotted turbans. The Rabari shepherd women of Kutch, in Gujarat, favour a completely black garb, tempered by *bandhani odhnis* in black wool minutely patterned in blood red and pricked with the sharp glitter of tiny fragments of mirror glass. The main centres of *bandhani* in Gujarat are Jamnagar, Porbander, Morvi, Rajkot, Bhuj and, especially, Mandvi. Fine tie-dyeing is also practised in the Rajasthani towns of Jaipur, Bikaner, Jodhpur, Ajmer, Udaipur and, most particularly, Sikar.

Another variety of colourful tie-dyed work exclusive to Jodhpur, Jaipur and Udaipur in Rajasthan is known as *laheria*, meaning waves, referring to its striped patterning. The vogue for elaborately tied *laheria* turbans was widespread in the nineteenth and early twentieth century as the distinguishing attire of the *marwaris*, the merchant and banking community of Rajasthan. Not limited by status nowadays, *laheria* cloth is a popular choice for turbans and *odhni*, and much imitated by mass-produced screen-printed textiles.

In true *laheria* dyeing the cotton cloth is rolled diagonally from corner to corner, and tied at the requisite intervals to create stripes. For a multi-coloured series of stripes, some sections of the rolled fabric are opened after the first dye bath, and fresh areas bound before dyeing the whole or part of the cloth in a fresh colour. Further complexity, resulting in a chequered pattern of intersecting diagonals, is achieved by folding between the other two corners and repeating the process. The *laheria* binding process, carried out by twisting and tying the cloth when wet on a short upright wooden pole, is exacting and exhausting work. Like *bandhani*, *laheria* is sold with the ties intact, as proof of its labour-intensive manufacture.

TIE-AND-DYE PROCESSES

Gujarat and Rajasthan are renowned for their textile traditions. The wave-patterned cottons, known as laheria, *are popular for use as turbans (opposite below). The preparation process involves the binding and dyeing of rolled lengths of cloth (opposite above). More widespread is the tying-and-dyeing of pin-prick patterns, whether on wool shawls (left) or fine cotton cloth (above).*

THE PRINTERS OF CLOTH

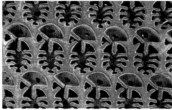

Sitting cross-legged at a low wooden table, this woman from Jodhpur, Rajasthan (centre left), will carefully overprint with a patterned wooden block many yards of cloth at a sitting. At a later stage, after the indigo bath, the fugitive yellow derived from turmeric is rubbed onto such yardage (opposite), which finds a ready market as skirt cloth for the women of the local farming communities.

Made to order all over northern India by specialist carvers, the printing blocks (left) are fashioned from hardwood, and are carved anew to an identical pattern when worn out. Such blocks display design influences from near and far.

THE CLOTH PRINTER

Like dyers, the textile printers of India are recognizable by their colour-splashed clothing and stained hands and arms. Unlike tie-dyeing, where an effective composition depends on the flair of the craftsman, the block printing of cloth is a repetitive business calling for dedicated precision. It is practised by both men and women. The prepared cloth is laid flat on the table or bench and the freshly dipped wooden block is pressed with the flat of the hand, reinforced by a delicate thump of the fist, each time adding an element to the complex interlocking pattern.

Cloth is hand-printed in India by two traditional means. Patterns may be created by first treating the cloth with a mordant that will react with dye applied to the printing block. Conversely, a similar block may be used to apply an impermeable resist – a material such as clay, resin or wax, or a paste made with gum – to define the areas that are not to be coloured. Once hand-printed, the material is dyed. As a final process, the resist is washed, brushed or melted off.

Working with such techniques and a multitude of combinations of processes using predominantly synthetic dyes, the block printers of India are, like dyers, necessarily found close by water: at a tank or pond as well as on a river bank. Concentrated in the northern and especially the north-western states of India, block printing is a craft of the village as well as of town and city. As with many a craft of India, production of such textiles in the larger towns is usually in the hands of the merchants. These men specify the kind of textile to be made and advance money to provide materials, such as the blocks for printing, cloth, dyes and mordants, to the groups of craftsmen specializing in each of the different operations. These craftsmen are contracted to complete the work at piece rates.

Today, the production of block-printed cotton textiles remains a handcrafted process, while vast quantities of patterned cotton and rayon are manufactured by machine printing. In the drive to compete in overseas markets, the machine printing industry and that of large-scale screen printing by hand has mushroomed since the last quarter of the nineteenth century. Many a town consumer and villager alike now prefers the synthetic mass-produced product, which is easy to wash and quick to dry, and much of this is now mechanically printed in patterns derived from those produced by wooden blocks. There remains, however, a local demand for block-printed cotton cloth which is used for unstitched garments, such as *lungis* (lower garments worn

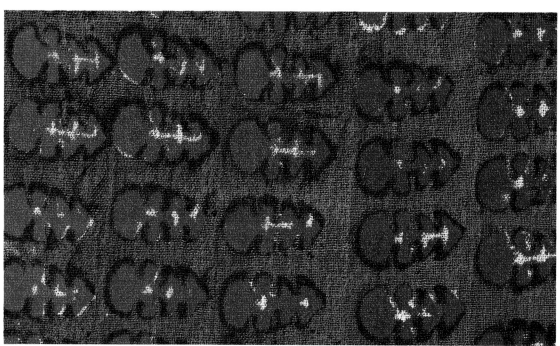

SIMPLE PRINTED CLOTH

For the Patel caste of farmers in Gujarat and Rajasthan, this pattern has become their hallmark (right). The design is known as panni hari, *'the woman who brings water'.*

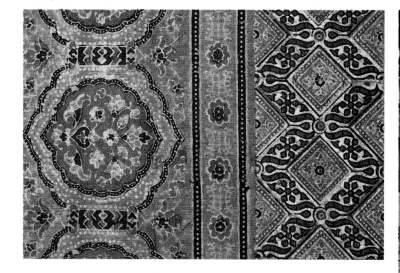

AJRAKH *CLOTH*

Produced in Kutch, as well as in Barmer, Rajasthan, is the exotically patterned cloth known as ajrakh *(above and right). This is a popular textile with both Hindus and Muslims, often worn on festive occasions as turbans or* lungis.

by men) and turbans or *pagri*, for women's saris and *odhnis*, as lengths for making up the *ghagra* or skirt and *choli* or blouse, and for floor and bed coverings. For the farming communities of Gujarat and Rajasthan, this handmade commercial production remains in great demand, and many a woman in each community proudly wears a skirt or *odhni* in a particular and exclusive printed pattern that is a mark of her status within the village.

The Gujarat region has always been one of the great textile exporters of India, with most of its goods produced by block printing. Early evidence of Gujarat's involvement in the international trade of colourful block-printed cloths comes from excavations in distant Egypt at Fostat, outside Cairo, which have yielded fragments of textiles dated to the fifteenth century. Extraordinarily, these had been resist-printed with unsophisticated but pleasing patterns that are typical of the hand-printed textiles of the region today. Historically centred on the regions of Saurashtra and Kutch, Gujarat remains an important source of printed cloth, in terms of both volume and quality. Towns and villages of the state well known for the craft include Surat, Broach, Baroda, Deesa, Ahmedabad, Rajkot, Jamnagar, Bhavnagar, Jetpur, Bhuj, Dhamadka, Khavda and Mundra.

Of these centres Ahmedabad, now a large industrial city, has a long association with the volume production of block-printed cloth in designs of floral sprays and simulated *bandhani* on a predominantly red background. In northern Gujarat, Deesa is also known for floral prints, but with traits characteristic of Persian and Mughal designs. Khavda and Dhamadka villages in Kutch, as well as Barmer in neighbouring Rajasthan, are known for printing the exotic rich blue and red cloth known as *ajrakh* – the name is thought to be derived from the Arabic for blue, *azrak*. These cloths are block-printed in a complicated sequence that involves both resist and mordant techniques. The prized deep blue sheen is derived from repeated dipping in indigo followed by vigorous beating and polishing; the most highly valued *ajrakh* are those printed on both sides. Sported by Muslim men and boys as festive wear for weddings and market days, and also popular with the Hindu *meghwal* caste of leather workers, *ajrakh* cloth is prepared in a variety of sizes to suit its traditional uses in turbans, *lungis* and shoulder cloths.

Rajasthan has a long and distinguished tradition of block printing, made familiar to many by the modern fashion export work of the printers and dyers of Sanganer and Bagru, near Jaipur. Originally it was their Mughal-inspired floral prints that brought wealth and fame to the area. Textiles from Sanganer were, on balance, more sophisticated, having a white or pale background decorated with colourful floral twigs or sprays. The Bagru printed cloths were originally prepared for the tastes of the local rural womenfolk, often comprising a light brown background spotted with the flowers and leaves of roses, vegetables, and herbs and spice plants. In recent years the merchants, dyers and printers of Bagru have become more adaptable and adventurous in their choice and use of a variety of block-printed designs, whereas Sanganer is now dominated by the screen-printing trade. Elsewhere in Rajasthan, the desert towns of Bikaner, Jodhpur, Barmer and Balotra continue to block-print traditional designs for the local rural women; Udaipur, Chittorgarh, Ajmer, Pipad and Kota are other centres renowned for the craft.

To the east, the textile colouring tradition continues with the block printers of Madhya Pradesh and Uttar Pradesh, and although these are less well known groups, they are active in the supply of cloth for local and national demand. On the western borders of Madhya Pradesh, the cloth-printing centres of Bagh, Ujjain, Mandsaur, Umedpura, Tarapur and Maheshwar belong to the southern Rajasthan and eastern Gujarat tradition of textile decoration. Gwalior, to the north, belongs to the Uttar Pradesh group of Agra and Mathura. Eastwards, along the Jamuna and Ganges rivers and their tributaries, lie the block-printing centres of Farrukhabad, Kanauj, Lucknow, Kanpur and Tanda; and to the south Allahabad, Benares and Mirzapur. In western Maharashtra there is a scattering of block-printing activity centred on Bombay, and in the east at Amravati, Saoner, Nagpur, Wani and Chandrapur.

THE *IKAT* MAKER

Known throughout the world as *ikat*, derived from the Malay word *mengikat* meaning to tie or bind, this is a complex and meticulous process in which, before the cloth is woven, the warp or weft threads, or both, are bundled and bound with threads or rubber bands that resist the action of dyestuffs. They are then repeatedly dyed to create bands of pattern. The weaving process itself is relatively simple. In India *ikat* is woven in Gujarat, Andhra Pradesh and Orissa, where it is often rather confusingly described as 'tie and dye' or *bandhani*, as well as being known by the specific and regional titles of *patola*, *mashru* and *telia rumal*. Whatever their titles, the quality of these *ikat* textiles is unsurpassed.

The contemporary *ikat* textiles of Andhra Pradesh and Orissa are woven by essentially the same technique as the more famous *patola* cloths of Gujarat, but the tools are quite different and the pit loom has been adapted in order to produce commercial quantities of *ikat* yardage with ease.

method. It is extraordinarily demanding and slow work, and a single sari may take more than a month to complete, so it is no wonder that *patola* is a cloth for the wealthy, often used for sumptuous marriage saris.

These double *ikats* were, however, an export success of the past, shipped to Malaya and Indonesia as early as the fifteenth century, where *patolas* were prized as the garb of the nobility and revered for their magical and sacred properties. To supply this trade there were once thriving industries of *patola* weaving at Ahmedabad, Cambay, Surat and Patan in Gujarat, as well as in neighbouring Maharashtra and Madhya Pradesh. Today two Jain families remain as the final practitioners of this art in Patan, Gujarat, producing a very limited output for discerning patrons. Their work continues the tradition of excellence in the preparation of the *patola*, as seen in their silk sari cloths with a traditional deep red or green ground, intricately patterned with an energetic lattice of white, blue and black designs of flowers, leaves and stars, around or within which animals, birds and humans are portrayed.

While the double *ikat* weaving tradition of Gujarat is in real danger of extinction, the *ikat* weavers of Orissa and Andhra Pradesh are thriving as never before. Inspired by the technical and marketing skills of their local government and co-operatives, these dyers and weavers have over the past forty years dominated the national handloom weaving market with well made, fashionably coloured and patterned, single and double *ikat* scarves, saris and furnishing fabrics. The dyeing and weaving of *ikat* in Orissa has tended to concentrate on the domestic unfitted garment market in silk and cotton, so that the *ikat* patterning is seen only on the borders and *muhun* or *pallav* (decorated endpiece or pieces) of saris and *dupattas* (shawls). Such work, often on a deep green, blue, brown, red or charcoal ground, includes such motifs as fish, swans and conch shells interspersed with bands of colour set with jewel-like abstracted floral and geometric designs.

In the districts of Sambalpur and Cuttack in Orissa and in the environs of the Andhra villages of Pochampalli, Chirala and Puttapaka there are now thousands of simple pit looms at work, often improved by the fitting of a flying shuttle, and working with *ikat*-dyed silk, cotton and synthetic yarns. Guided by the enthusiastic and well organized Government Handloom Service Centres and spurred on by their own contacts with merchants and traders from home and abroad, the Orissa, and particularly the Andhra, weavers are directly copying as well as interpreting the textile compositions from other *ikat* dyeing and weaving sources, including Gujarat, as well as patterns from foreign cultures, such as Japan and Central America.

The oldest tradition of *ikat* weaving is probably that of Gujarat state. Medieval writings reverently praise the silk *patola* of the region, the name deriving from the Sanskrit *pattakula*, meaning silk cloth. The preparation of the complex and colourful patterning of the *patola* involves the dyeing of both the warp and the weft yarns. After arranging the warps on the simple loom frame to create the transverse stripes of the composition, the wefts, arranged in sequence on bobbins, are interlaced in plain weave so that the colours meet and blend to create the desired design. Two weavers work together on a loom tilted at an angle of about thirty degrees from the horizontal so that they can readily keep an eye on the work. They can adjust the interlacing of the threads with a pencil-like metal rod to keep the pattern in order. Designs and compositions of remarkable intricacy are possible by this

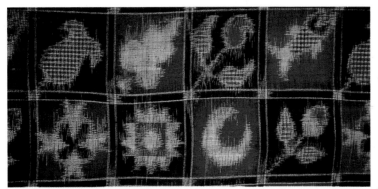

THE CHIRALA WEAVERS

The square ikat textiles of Chirala, Andhra Pradesh, are known as telia rumals (from the oily smell and feel of the alizarin dye) or Asia rumals. Today, the few surviving weavers of Chirala supply the local fishermen, who use the telia rumals (left) as turbans.

THE SPINNING WHEEL

Throughout India the hand-powered floor spinning wheel is known as a charka. Using the wool from the family's flock of sheep, this woman from the Thar desert of Rajasthan (opposite) teases, twists and then ties yarn onto a horizontally mounted spindle shaft, which is wound by a string attached to the spoked wheel. The wheel is spun, thus charging the spindle with yarn.

THE IKAT WEAVERS OF ANDHRA PRADESH AND ORISSA

The complex and meticulous dyeing and weaving process whereby yarn is bound with threads or rubber bands, and then repeatedly dyed before being woven (above), is known throughout the world as ikat. For the women of Orissa, a favoured cloth for a sari is the cotton ikat known as bandha, found in deep

tones of blue, red and magenta. These examples (right and centre), filled with auspicious symbols such as fish and the mythical swan, are made in Orissa at Nuapatna, near Cuttack on the coastal plain, or in the weaving centres inland around the towns of Sambalpur and Sonepur.

THE WEAVER

The noise of the handloom is often heard in the back streets of cities, towns and villages throughout India, adding to the general cacophony a sound of vitality and enterprise that provokes the imagination, and yet soothes the senses with its rhythm. This heartbeat of creativity extends to the gentle welcome that is always accorded any visitor to the home or workshop of a weaver and his family. There, sitting with a cup of tea, one may enjoy the busy sound and sight of the weavers at work − the rustle and shake of the moving heddles, the swing and thump of the reed as it compacts the weave, and the whir or clack of the flying shuttles flashing back and forth. Looms range from the simplest imaginable to complex semi-mechanized treadle machines. Across the length and breadth of India handweavers turn out a multiplicity of textiles for traditional and fashionable garments, for home and export.

Aside from very simple looms such as the single heddle type used by the Patan *patola* weavers, the narrow loom used for the weaving of Rajasthani camel girths, and the backstrap looms of the tribal peoples of the north-eastern states and Orissa, the commonest and simplest weaving apparatus is the pit loom. This is so named because it is strung out on the ground. The treadles, or pedals, which move the heddles therefore have to be sunk in a pit in the earth floor of the house or work area. To operate these the weaver sits on the ground or a low bench, and dangles his legs into the pit. Just above his thighs the breast beam and simple frame of the loom are set on wooden supports, which extend upwards to carry the heddles. These are transverse beams carrying rows of 'leashes', strings connected to the warp threads. The heddles and leashes are moved up and down by the treadles, opening a gap or 'shed' between two groups of warp threads through which the shuttle carrying the weft thread is thrown − either by hand or, in the case of a 'flying' shuttle, by a simple mechanism. A wood-framed 'reed' or cloth beater, pivoted on the frame, is driven against each newly inserted weft thread to keep the weave tight and even. The warps are either unwound from a revolving warp beam as the cloth progresses, or they are gathered and tied to a post, from which they are unravelled from time to time by a young assistant. Producing textiles ranging from plain white hand-spun cotton *khadi* cloth to the single *ikat* furnishing cloth of Andhra Pradesh, this simple treadle loom, and its slightly more mechanized variants, is the most popular weaving apparatus.

The textile craftsmen of India have, however, taken the simple act of weaving to a high art of complexity and variation. From

the fundamental process of plain weaving, merely passing the weft threads over one warp thread and under the next, the weaver of the subcontinent has evolved a panoply of indigenous techniques to create cloth. These range from twills in which weft threads 'float' or pass over two warps at once, through tabby, rep and satin weaves with longer floats to complex tapestry patterns and the insertion of supplementary wefts or warps to create rich brocades. Add to this mix of weaving possibilities a vast choice of fine-quality cottons − at least twenty-three varieties − as well as a multitude of silks, rayons and precious metal threads, and it is no wonder that India has been a world centre of textile production for thousands of years.

Although the pit loom continues to be the backbone of the Indian handloom weaving industry, it has been the evolution of more complex types, with multiple heddles that lift the warp threads in different groups, that has enabled the weaver to practise a multitude of patterning techniques. Since the early decades of this century many looms have also been modernized by the addition of extra shafts and pattern rods operated by hand for the insertion of supplementary wefts and, less commonly, supplementary warps. More often than not a father and his son

THE WEAVING OF SHAWLS

Across India a variety of looms is used to weave all manner of cloth. For the cold winter nights of Gujarat and Rajasthan the woollen, or wool and cotton, blanket-like shawl (above) is popular amongst the pastoral communities. Bhujodi in Kutch is a centre for weaving, importing wool from Russia as well as Maharashtra and using simple pit looms (left). Popular patterns include a cream ground with vivid coloured borders and patterned end panels. The Rabari, however, favour all-black headshawls.

For the cold winters of the Himalayas many layers of woollen and padded cotton clothing are necessary. In Ladakh a primitive framed treadle loom (right) produces strips of woven sheeps' wool, which are then made up into a variety of warm garments.

or daughter will work such a labour-intensive pit loom, the child inserting the extra wefts with a small bobbin of coloured or metal thread. In this manner the skills and traditions of weaving become second nature to the children of a weaving family.

Many of the most highly prized saris are woven on such relatively simple looms. Some of these textiles are valued for their glittering quality, as with heavily brocaded and weighty silk cloth laden with gold and silver thread; and others, conversely, for their translucent quality, as with muslin, which floats on the body like a mist of ethereal and delicate floral patterning. Of the former, Benares is the most famous source of the metal-thread patterned cloth called *zari*, as well as of the exceedingly elaborate gold brocades known as *kinkhab*, or 'little dream', which are often used for wedding saris. By contrast to the bustle of such an ancient metropolis, pockets of weavers continue to thrive in the rural areas of India, working fine brocades to the commissioned orders

of far-off merchants. In Maharashtra, for example, the village of Paithan is renowned for the use of silk-patterned, rather than metal, brocade work to decorate the endpiece and borders of saris. Worked on a golden background are brocaded patterns of parrots, geese and flowers in deep hues of green, yellow, blue and red silks. Other centres of metal-thread brocade weaving are spread across the whole country and include Murshidabad in West Bengal, Surat and Ahmedabad in Gujarat, Maheshwar and Chanderi in Madhya Pradesh, Mysore in Karnataka and Kanchipuram and Thanjavur in Tamil Nadu.

The most famous of the fine and lightweight patterned cloths are the *jamdani* cottons, traditionally woven in Dacca, as well as Tanda in Uttar Pradesh. There, the looms used are simple and the pattern detailing laborious, for true *jamdani* work requires a delicate touch and dexterity of the highest order. Seated at the loom, the master and his assistant weave patterns with

FINE SILK AND COTTON WEAVING

Many of the most highly prized textiles, such as this silk sari (opposite) from Orissa and the brocaded textile from Maharashtra (below right) are woven on simple pit looms with extra heddles. In Benares, a city famous for its production of heavily brocaded silk cloth, semi-mechanized looms (right) facilitate the intricate work.

The fine muslins and silks woven in the Gangetic basin of northern India have been in demand since classical times. The most famous of these is the jamdani *cotton, woven at Dacca in Bangladesh as well as in West Bengal and Uttar Pradesh. In* jamdani *work the weft floral patterns appear to float within the cloth, rather than acting as a surface decoration as with brocade. Of a similar lightweight nature is the silk cloth of Baluchar, West Bengal, known as* butidar *(left).*

coloured or metal thread by following paper patterns of the designs laid under the warps, aided by lilting verbal instructions. The *jamdani* technique is essentially tapestry work, as wefts form the pattern where needed and are threaded through the warps with a bamboo needle, rather than in a shuttle or on a bobbin. By using the lightest of yarn, the weft patterns of paisley and floral sprigs appear to merge with and float within the cloth, rather than appearing as an overlay of woven decoration. Of a similar featherweight nature is the silk cloth of Baluchar in West Bengal, where the weavers use a *jamdani* loom to create dark red and purple saris decorated with brocaded designs of small flowers (*butis*) in yellow and orange hues. From these floral motifs the name of the cloth, known as *butidar*, is derived. In Bengal the decorated end section of the sari is known as an *anchal* rather than a *pallav*, and in *butidar* cloth this is often boldly patterned with figurative scenes.

Carpet weaving is a most important export and domestic trade for the merchants of Agra, Bhadohi and Mirzapur in Uttar Pradesh, as well as those of Jaipur in Rajasthan, and in the Kashmir Valley. Raised to a level of technical and creative excellence by the Mughal courts at Delhi, Lahore and Agra, the carpet weavers of today are more than capable of meeting the needs of a thriving international market for these decorative and functional floor rugs.

Following in the wake of this highly successful Indian knotted carpet trade, however, is the recent rise of interest in the flat-woven cotton rugs known as *dhurries*. These inexpensive textiles are made on primitive ground looms and have been used over the centuries in homes throughout India, varying in size and grandeur from the gargantuan palace-commissioned *dhurries* to the small bed and prayer *dhurries*, which are used by the town dweller and villager alike.

In the mansions and palaces of the wealthy, such *dhurries* were often used as underlay to protect the more valuable carpets on top. The largest often extended to over 25 metres in length and 10 metres in width. Smaller *dhurries* are more commonly found. The prayer *dhurrie* varies according to Muslim or Hindu custom: Muslim rugs, for example, are often woven in long strips each containing the shape of a prayer niche indicating the direction of Mecca. Bed *dhurries*, made of thick cotton, are usually out of sight, sandwiched between the wooden frame of the bed and the mattress. The simple floor *dhurrie* is most familiar in the West. All these types of *dhurrie* were made to the highest standards, often in the jails of colonial India from the late nineteenth to the early twentieth century, and commissions from the local gentry and expatriates, which derived from traditional compositions and floor-tile patterns, resulted in a range of decorative floor rugs of great variety.

Dhurries are 'weft faced' – that is, the weft threads form the most visible part of the surface – and their patterning techniques are much the same as those of any tapestry weave the world over: slit work, dovetailing, double interlocking, eccentric wefts and weft float patterning. Compositions can vary enormously, especially in recent years, but most have either mimicked or interpreted the floral and geometric combinations of Persian and Turkish carpets, or followed the simple and soothing character of bands and large blocks of plain colour that are the hallmark of all vernacular tapestry-weaving cultures. In the villages of Karnataka, the Punjab, Haryana and Rajasthan *dhurrie* weaving continues on the whole to be a family craft, whereas there is a thriving, international designer-inspired export industry in flat weaves centred on Agra and Fatehpur Sikri in the north, and Coimbatore and Salem in the south.

COTTON FLAT WEAVES

The making of flat weave cotton rugs, or dhurries, is a form of weaving found in many states of India (right). The craft was given added encouragement in Rajasthan as the local nobility found dhurries ideal for covering the vast expanses of marble palace floors.

DHURRIE *WEAVERS OF RAJASTHAN*

As flat woven rugs increase in popularity outside India, so the dhurrie weavers have found a new breed of patron. Working on simple ground looms in a courtyard (far left), or shaded under a makeshift awning, these Rajasthani village weavers are creating dhurries to the orders of European and American merchants. Many compositions are inspired by the motifs and patterns of Turkish or Persian flat weaves, known as kilims, and coloured to match the decorative fashions of the day. Whereas the patterns are always evolving, the techniques and tools used have altered little over the centuries (opposite above and left).

THE EMBROIDERER

The ornamentation of woven cloth with needle and thread in embroidery stitches and appliqué is an ancient tradition of the subcontinent. And it is a tradition that is particularly associated with the tribes and peoples of Kashmir, the Punjab, Rajasthan and Gujarat.

Of these regions Gujarat was, from the seventeenth century and for over 200 years, the world's most important source of fine commercial needlework; and the direct inheritors of the tradition, the professional embroiderers of the *mochi* and *meghwal* leather-working communities, continue to ply their trade in the region today. Working in, and selling from, their backstreet workshops, they devote themselves mostly to the embroidery and construction of the leather shoes sold to the local farmers and fashionable tourists alike. There is also a lively trade in the upholstery of metal and wooden camel saddles, a craft that includes the making up of bespoke padded hide cushions with an embroidery inset of bright floral motifs. Away from the towns, however, in the villages and nomadic shelters of the farmers and shepherds of the region, there continues to exist a needleworking tradition that has produced delightful folk embroideries.

The Kutch and Saurashtra provinces of Gujarat, as well as south-western Rajasthan and the adjoining province of Sind in Pakistan, share a rich inheritance of shared folk embroidery traditions which centre on the dowry. In addition to the usual gifts of jewellery and household utensils, a bride will bring to her new husband's home a wealth of richly embroidered textiles carefully worked by herself and the women of her family. Such a dowry often consists of costumes for the bride and groom, hangings for their new home and trappings for their domestic animals; all decorated with embroidery that is often highlighted by the sparkle of small mirrors, known as *shisha*.

Carried from the bride's family home to that of her new parents-in-law wrapped in a large, square embroidered cloth (*chakla*) or stuffed into a dowry bag (*khotri*), the textile dowry, particularly that of the *kathi* farming community, includes several kinds of colourfully embroidered household hangings. As a welcome to visitors and gods alike, an embroidered frieze known as a *toran* is hung above the doorway, its hanging pennants representing mango leaves, considered symbols of good luck. To either side are hung two L-shaped embroideries known as *sankia*, accompanied by smaller friezes, or *pantoran*, as well as the square *chakla* which also serves as a hanging.

Although the display of embroidery as a token of wealth takes pride of place at the protracted wedding celebrations, the

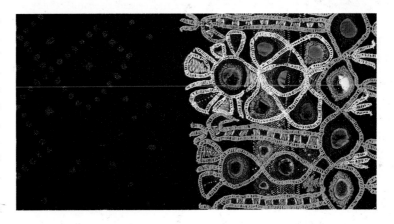

EMBROIDERERS OF KUTCH

For the finest and most prolific source of folk embroideries in the world, the scrublands of Kutch and Kathiawar in Gujarat are arguably without peer. Devoted to the decoration of clothing and houses alike, the embroideries of the pastoral communities such as the Ahir and Rabari are now collected and sold worldwide, whether in their orignal forms such as the doorway frieze or toran (opposite) or cut up and made into garments and bags. The embroideries are always filled with auspicious floral motifs (above) as well as figurative subjects (top) such as the ever popular elephants, parrots and tortoises.

METAL-THREAD EMBROIDERY OF UTTAR PRADESH

In a separate tradition to the folk embroideries of Gujarat and Rajasthan are the metal-thread costumes and accessories (detail below) made in such centres as Vrindaban and Mathura. For the staging of the raslila *plays, these two boys (right) are adorned with metal-thread headdresses to represent Krishna and his consort Radha.*

needlework tradition also brings colour, identity and symbolism to everyday life. Each farming caste and community of the region will proudly wear embroidered clothes as a distinctive uniform, and every group has its own particular style of needlework, range of colours and repertoire of stitches. In the full skirts, shawls and blouses worn by the young women and children there are vivid contrasts of colour in happy combinations of vermilion, acid green, black, orange and blue, all of which combine with the embroidery patterns to create a welcome and exciting visual respite from the dun landscapes of the region.

This embroidery tradition, as elsewhere in India, is predominantly the work of the women, young and old, who delight in covering a plain cotton ground with a range of figurative, floral and geometric patterns according to their religious observance. In recent years, however, many communities have either turned to the more remunerative and largely lifeless production of floral-patterned needlework lengths, bags and stitched garments for the fashion trade or have ceased their dowry work altogether, following the fashion for dowries of consumer goods and cash. Of those groups for whom an embroidered trousseau remains a traditional requirement, the Rabari shepherd families of Kutch are the most striking and elegant. Seen pacing the streets of a market town with lissome poise, the Rabari women often reveal a brief glimpse of the bright embroidered colours of a blouse and skirt beneath the dark and mysterious shawls in which they envelope themselves.

Among the other embroidery communities of India, the yellow, red and orange shawls known as *phulkari* (flower work) and *bagh* (garden), which comprise the dowry needlework of the Punjabi farming women, are renowned, as well as the *rumals*, or cowrie-shell edged handkerchiefs, and money and betel-nut purses of the itinerant Banjara of central India; for both groups such stitchery remains an active occupation. Heavily collected by museums, galleries and tourists alike, their work is inevitably tending to lose much of its original charm and identity.

Masterful work of the relatively recent past is still echoed in the weaves and embroideries of Himachal Pradesh, Kashmir and Bengal. The tapestry weaving of shawls in the Kashmir Valley is now a memory, replaced by the stem-, feather- and chain-stitch work of the professional male embroiderers, who decorate plain wool with paisley motifs, Mughal arches and a variety of pleasing leaves and flowers. In Bengal, the once great *kantha* tradition by which old saris and dhotis were embroidered and quilted with naive charm has now returned, though on a small scale, while in Chamba, Himachal Pradesh, the lively representations of mythological characters and courtly life seen on old embroidered silk and cotton *rumals* have also been revived.

EMBROIDERED SADDLES AND SHOES

The professional leather workers and cobblers of western India are known as the Mochi community. Found tucked away in a tiny workshop in many a backstreet, these craftsmen and women shape, stitch and embroider leather goods such as camel saddle cushions (left) and brightly decorated shoes (below), a popular form of footwear with local farmers.

POTTERY

PAST INSPIRATION

Simple in shape and archaic in decoration, the water and curd pots (above) of Bhuj in Kutch have evolved little since antiquity. Far to the south, this master craftsman of Karigiri in Tamil Nadu (left) turns the initial form for a decorative glazed water container using ancient skills once inspired by Muslim patronage.

The work of the potter is so much a part of India's everyday round of work and worship that, assured of his reliable and productive skill, the Aryan scriptures give no honorific titles to his kind, no complex social stratification as they do to other craftsmen. Yet it is this very quality of unassuming, patient creativity, stretching back in an unbroken line to pre-history, that distinguishes the craftsman in clay from his fellow artists.

The potter participates in a rhythmical vocation that takes the substance of the earth itself, gives it form as it rises from the centre of a spinning wheel, and creates an object of beauty which, after a life of daily utility, will be returned to the soil before being regenerated into new forms. It is no wonder, therefore, that so many tales are told of the potter's origin, histories and virtues, foremost among which is his popular title, that of Prajapati, the Lord of the People, said to have been awarded by Brahma himself when breathing life into a clay form to create man. The potters still retain a respect for the divine origins of their craft. Every day, before the potter sets to work, his simple tools are given due veneration as gifts from god, and prayers are offered for the hands to be guided by the lord.

THE POTTER OF INDIA

Throughout India the usual name by which the potter is known is *kumbhar*, and there are two explanations for the origin of this designation. A legend describes how elephants bathing in the river would delight in sloshing cool water and mud over their heads. The mud, settling in the hollow of the forehead, would dry to leave a clay shape which the people found useful as a plate or dish. The head of an elephant is called *kumbha*, and so the potters who imitated the clay form were named after it. Another tells of the marriage ceremony of Shiva and Parvati, during which an earthenware vessel (*kumbha*) was required. A Brahman threw a pot using the sacred discus of Vishnu as a wheel, Mount Mandar as a pivot and Shiva's pestle as a turning tool. His progeny became the potters of this world. A less diverting explanation relates to its Sanskrit derivation. The prefix *ku* means 'of the earth', and a clay pitcher is therefore called *kumbha*. Regional variations of the potter's name include *kumbhakara* and *kumar*, and in the Dravidian south *kovara* in Kanarese, *kummara* in Telugu, and *kusavan* in Tamil and Malayalam.

Evidence of continuity in the products of the potter is not hard to come by. Finds from pre-Harappan and more recent periods have much in common with the work of the present day. At Kalibangan in Rajasthan 4000-year-old wares were found, painted in black and white on a red ground with a predominantly geometric patterning, and direct parallels may be drawn between this style and the modern work of the potters of Bhuj in Kutch. Likewise, artefacts found at Mohenjo Daro have included clay rattles, whistles, animals, dolls and sundry toys amid the everyday storage and cooking vessels, making up a stock that would not be out of place in the potters' compound of many an Indian village in the late twentieth century.

So profound is this spirit of continuity in the potter's art that the craft remains largely unsullied by the influence of the modern world. The potter's products, fragile, cheap and bulky, still restrict his market to the immediate vicinity despite recent improvements in transportation. Unlike the majority of the craftsmen of India, therefore, he remains largely untouched by the changing fashions of the national and international market. And while he has not benefited from the cultural infusions and transplantations that have inspired his associates, he succeeds eminently in the continuous honing of simple and beautiful skills. Channelling his talents through his fingers to the clay on the wheel or in his hand, the potter labours, now as ever, to satisfy two distinct roles within the community: that of purveyor of everyday household wares, and maker of votive objects.

THE POTTER AT WORK

Whether travelling through the lands of Mithila in Bihar to find the lamp makers at work (opposite above and below) or seeking the craftsmen in the village of Molela in Rajasthan (left), any meeting with a potter of India might well recall the following words of Ananda Coomaraswamy: 'The Indian craftsman conceives of his art, not as the accumulated skill of ages but originating in the divine skill of Viśvakarma (God of creation), and as revealed by him. Beauty, rhythm, proportion, idea have an absolute existence on an ideal plane, where all who seek may find. The reality of things exists in the mind, not in the detail of their appearance to the eye. Their inward inspiration, upon which the Indian artist is taught to rely, appearing like a still small voice of a god, and that god was conceived of as Viśvakarma. He may be thought of as that part of divinity which is conditioned by a special relation to artistic expression; or in another way, as the sum total of consciousness, the group soul of the individual craftsmen of all times and places... Under such conditions, the craftsman is not an individual expressing individual whims, but a part of the universe, giving expression to the ideals of eternal beauty and unchanging laws, even as do the trees and flowers whose natural and less ordered beauty is no less God-given.'

The Indian Craftsman. A. K. Coomaraswamy. London, 1909.

TERRACOTTA PANELS AND STORAGE JARS

Seen within a mudwalled and thatched Rabari hut, forming the front of a whitewashed cupboard (top), this decorative clay moulding is the handiwork of the village women of the Kutch and Saurashtra regions of Gujarat

(above left). For the storage of pulses and grain, unfired and whitewashed clay jars (above), seen behind a Rajasthani carpenter at work, are made by the building-up of successive coils of clay.

THE MAKER OF HOUSEHOLD WARES

The variety of utilitarian wares produced by the potter of India is extraordinary, and yet none shows any gratuitous decoration or shaping beyond the desire to make the object functional and attractive in the eyes of god, as well as the customer. In most regions the potter's wheel remains the predominant means of

densely populated Gangetic plain and the south, a group of potters is clustered along an entire street. Some of these communities form a complete potters' hamlet or suburb to the main village; in this way not only is the need for segregation satisfied, but the concentration of business attracts more customers. The potter's house includes a courtyard and often extends over quite an area, for there must be ample room for the storage of clay, an open space for a kiln and as large a storage site as possible for pots to 'season', or dry in the sun before firing, and for the finished wares. Visiting a potter's home during the monsoon season, when the wheel is necessarily still, one views the expanse of deserted yard with surprise; yet a few weeks later, to meet the demands of Diwali, the Festival of Lamps, the same yard is densely arrayed with lamps and pots set out to dry, which compete for space with the completed work ready to go to market.

The actual work area is surprisingly confined, often nestling tight in the corner of an open courtyard, or a shaded verandah. There are few tools to clutter this space, and the centrepiece, the heavy wheel or *chak*, is placed out of the way against a wall when work is over. Wheels are usually made of wood or sun-baked clay, sometimes of local stone. Wooden wheels are centred on a spoked disc whose boss, the *thala*, and arms are handed down ceremoniously from generation to generation; the rim is renewed when necessary, secured by a binding of ropes and made smooth and well balanced with a covering of clay. When the wheel is set on its axle in the floor ready for the work of the day, it is an astonishing sight, whether on the first or the hundredth occasion, to watch the potter or his assistant whip it into action with a staff of wood. By placing this stick against a spoke or a recess on the flat surface, and stirring dexterously and vigorously, the wheel is 'wound up' with energy and spins in complete silence for what seems an age. The taciturn, but gentle and friendly potter at once takes a lump of clay and sets to work.

His other tools are equally simple: for applying a design on the wheel a finger or suitable twig serve perfectly well, although those working on surface-decorated wares or plaques will have a small basket of stone dies for stamping repeated motifs. For cutting the finished object from the wheel, a string or wire suffices, and this is often also used as a tool for decoration. Placed casually to one side, there may be a collection of small wooden bats, worn concave with use, accompanied by a pile of stone tappers that are shaped rather like flattened pestles. When creating a capacious water vessel, the potter can either form two or more sections for later assembly or throw a small, thick pot of the requisite shape that can then be enlarged, when partly dry, by 'tapping'. This process involves sitting before the prepared pot, which is resting in a cloth-covered bowl or broken pot base, and

forming and decoration; yet the work of some minorities, such as the tribal and Himalayan peoples, includes techniques such as modelling on an old pot, coiling, or slab construction and hand beating, and these methods continue to thrive.

There are more than a million potters in India, most of them in the villages, where more than eighty per cent of the nation's population reside and work. As a member of the lower echelons of society, the potter's home and workplace is likely to be found on the perimeter of the village; sometimes, as is common in the holding one of the tappers to the inside to brace the surface of the pot. The wooden bat is then slapped against the same place on the outside of the pot. The inertia of the heavy tapper prevents the blow from driving the wall of the pot in; instead, this is thinned, and the pot begins to bulge outwards. In this manner the entire vessel is enlarged ready for the final firing.

For his clay the potter must look to a local supply, to be found in a nearby river bed, lake, pond or tank. Some collect clay once a year in bulk by cart or lorry, but the majority make more frequent collections in baskets or sacks, sometimes carried by donkey or ox cart, sometimes on the heads of the entire family. The nature of the clay obviously varies tremendously: clay from Kutch in Gujarat is grey and soft, whereas in southern India it often has a bronze colour and is strong but lacks plasticity. The colour ranges from off-white through yellow, red, brown and grey to black. To create a terracotta hue to satisfy the customer's expectations, unsuitable-coloured vessels are often rubbed or painted with a red ochre slip before firing.

Before any moulding may begin, however, the raw clay must be cleansed of foreign bodies such as pebbles, roots and twigs, and any deficiencies in its texture that would make it hard to work are made good by adding sand, ashes, cow dung, grain husks or cotton wool. The aim is to create a compound that will be easy to handle and yet will not crack when drying in the sun or cooking in the kiln, or *bhatti*. As often as necessary a quantity of this dry mix will be soaked, and kneaded by hands and feet to give a dough-like consistency ready for the throwing or hand assembly of a vessel. The finished wares – and here it must be stressed that the vast majority of Indian pots are unglazed – are either left rough or polished when wet with smooth stones, or with the wooden mallet also used for tapping. All are then left in the yard to dry out in the sun to a firm consistency before being fired. Coloured decoration, where used, is usually applied to the pots just before firing.

The kilns of different villages, districts and regions vary enormously, but almost all are built to be fired on an 'open' principle. In its form, as may be seen beside many a main street in a potters' village in southern India, the pots to be fired are gingerly piled into an elongated mound, interlaced with firewood and cakes of cow-dung fuel before being covered with straw and dried grass. This tumulus is set ablaze and, as the contents cook, more grass is thrown on to the glowing heap. Some kilns consist of a quarter-circle of brick wall, others of a pit in the ground; but the fuels used remain similar, although in places where wood is scarce and expensive it may have to be replaced wholly or partly with wood shavings or even old tyres. To insulate and compact the mound of fuel, large pieces of broken pot may be

used, demonstrating again the cyclical nature of a potter's work.

The Indian potter's craft is not confined to the production of household vessels. In Raigarh and Sarguja in Madhya Pradesh and Sambalpur in Orissa, the potters make roof tiles, competing for the attention of their clients by decorating the tops of their ridge tiles with a zoo of frolicking animals, birds and mythological creatures. On the whitewashed interior and exterior walls of the home, the clay-moulding handiwork of many a village woman of the Kutch and Saurashtra districts in Gujarat is proudly exhibited. Working the clay by hand, they decorate walls, free-standing containers and shelves in relief with elaborately linked geometric and floral motifs, enlivened by representations of animals and birds and interspersed with the bright reflections of a scattering of tiny inset mirrors. A similar decorative practice

FROM KILN TO MARKET

For the potters of India the annual cycle of festivals and fairs, as well as everyday ritual and utility, provide a dynamic impetus to their work. Save during the monsoon period, when the potter's wheel stands idle and the sites for the open-air kilns are often a morass of mud, these craftsmen are hard at work providing an enormous range of pots and votive artefacts for the local communities. Before Diwali, the Festival of Lamps, the village potters prepare thousands of small bowls (opposite) for use as lamps (above). At Pongal, the Indian harvest festival, many households in the south buy new cooking and water pots for the year ahead. These are fired in open kilns (left) stacked with cow cakes and covered with straw.

is common to the villages of the Mandla district in Madhya Pradesh and the Madhubani area in Bihar, where the mud-walled exteriors of the huts are studded with clay representations of birds and cows, and circular and star motifs. These are renewed every year, especially during the festival season.

Entering into the comparative gloom of a village hut from the bright day outside, one is often aware of the looming presence of tall, bulbous vessels. These are the household storage jars for grain, foodstuffs and seeds. Sometimes as tall as four metres high, the hut is built around them. Made by the family by the patient and successive application of coils of clay, these unbaked vessels are frequently divided into compartments within, and decorated with gaudy colours and patterns without. For the supply of everyday terracotta wares, however, the family will turn to the local potter. This is often still a relationship dependent on barter. In the past there was a formal system of exchange known as *gara*, which is still sometimes practised. The supply of pots to the families of the village, and often the nearby settlements, would be apportioned between the local potters and remain a right from generation to generation. In return the potter would receive grain, other foodstuffs and money.

To meet the needs of such clients the village potter must be able to turn his hand to the production of an enormous variety of simple wares. The shape of each dish, plate, pot and vessel has evolved to match a use: pots for the carrying and storing of water, for holding oil, preserving pickles, making and keeping yoghurt and butter; cooking vessels for milk, rice and vegetables; griddles for all the varieties of unleavened bread; and the cooking stoves themselves. While the market is dominated by the supply of supremely elegant undecorated and unglazed terracotta goods, in every region there are exceptions of the most pleasing character. From Kutch in Gujarat, and especially from around the town of Bhuj, comes a range of cooking and food storage pots painted in red, black and white with geometric, floral and animal patterns. Nizamabad in Uttar Pradesh is famous for the lustrous black finish of its tall oil and water jars. Before firing the surface of the vessel is washed with a slip of powdered mango bark, yellow earth and soda, burnished with mustard oil and then decorated with incised patterns (*naqashi*) of floral sprays done with a pointed twig. To create a lustrous black sheen the pots are smoke-fired in a closed kiln, and the decoration completed by filling the grooves with a fine silvery amalgam, *bukani*, composed of lead, zinc and mercury. The finished pot has a most distinctive appearance, with a close affinity to the decorated black metalware of India, such as *bidri* work.

The creation of an impervious surface is addressed by many potters. In Dausa, Rajasthan, the highly polished black ware is

DECORATING UNGLAZED POTTERY

The great majority of Indian terracotta artefacts and utensils are fired without a glaze, and of these the bulk remain undecorated. The exceptions are the archaic patterning of cooking and storage vessels (below) by the wives of the potters of Bhuj in Kutch. The incised blackware (bottom) is a speciality of the district of Nagaur in Rajasthan and its semi-porous coated finish makes it popular with the local women for use as cooking pots. These potters are also well known for throwing, moulding and slab-forming a variety of whimsical toys as well as deities. After a wash of white slip, these trinkets and effigies are brush painted with colourful decorations (opposite below).

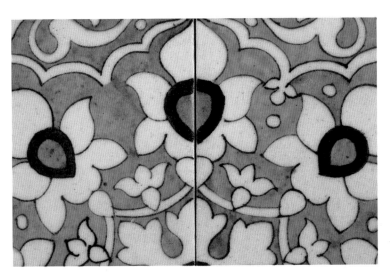

suitable for the preservation of oil and ghee; such pots are in constant demand from a wide range of communities in the region. The Bhil women of Chhota Udaipur in Gujarat are well known for their coating of terracotta surfaces with shellac, another solution to the problem of permeability. The melted shellac is applied to the interior of the fired vessel while it is still warm to give a smooth surface.

THE MAKER OF GLAZED WARES

Inspired by the techniques of the Mughal tile makers, the Kashmir Valley potters glaze their products to make them impermeable – a practice familiar to Western craftsmen. Their vessels are colourfully decorated, often with clusters of flowers.

The use of blue glaze on pottery, an imported technique, is believed to have been introduced to northern India during the fourteenth century by the early Muslim potentates. This technique in turn had been made possible by Mongol craftsmen, who brought together Chinese glazing technology and the Persian decorative arts. At first used in the making of tiles with which to decorate mosques, tombs and palaces in mimicry of their beloved effigies over the mountains in Central Asia, it was by way of the late Mughal regime that 'blueware' began to be applied more widely. The making of glazed wares centred on Delhi, and spread to the city of Jaipur in the early seventeenth century. In the creation of this splendid city the manufacture of glazed tiles enjoyed vigorous patronage, but then almost disappeared once the project had been completed. The revival of tile making began in the late nineteenth century with the founding of the Jaipur School of Art and, more recently, a thriving new industry producing a range of blueware has been established.

BLUE-GLAZED POTTERY OF JAIPUR

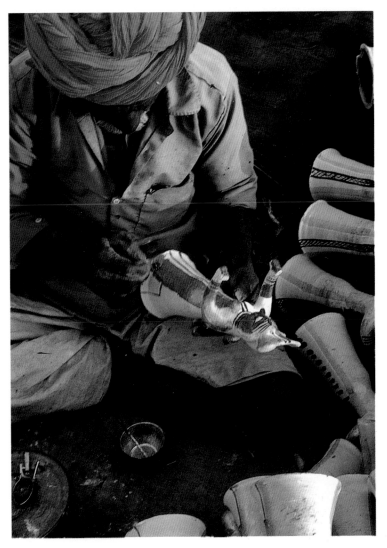

The impressive Rambagh Palace of Jaipur in Rajasthan, erstwhile home to Maharajas, is now a luxury hotel as are many royal palaces of the region. Happily, it is now possible to view their striking architecture and the accompanying decorative arts so beloved of the ruling Rajputs, from murals to inlaid semi-precious stones and mirror work. The rulers of Jaipur were especially fond of the blue-glazed ware that was introduced to north India by the Mughals from China by way of Persia and many a cool marble hall has as its centrepiece a bubbling fountain lined with ravishing blue tiles such as these (above left).

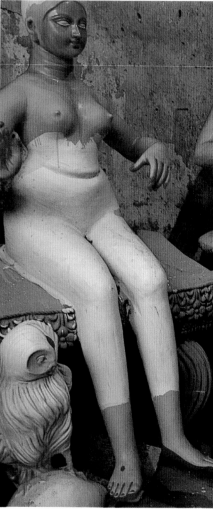

THE IDOL MAKER

THE EFFIGY MAKERS OF CALCUTTA

As the monsoon rains begin to slacken, and the skies turn from grey to a thin blue, the first major festival of the cooler season is celebrated. Known as Dussehra, it is a time when the power of good is proclaimed over evil. For the peoples of West Bengal and eastern Bihar the worship of the goddess Durga is prevalent. Within this region Calcutta is the centre of such festivities and fantastic temporary shrines are built throughout the city to house the gaily painted effigies of the deities. These figures, many over two metres tall, are made of straw and string (far left), coated with clay (left). Then, as with these figures of the goddess Saraswati (above and overleaf left) they are painted with layers of lurid paint, covered in varnish and adorned with clothing and garlands. The repeated beatific expressions of the models derive from a plaster mould (overleaf right).

Few Indian potters devote themselves exclusively to the making of idols in clay. Almost all potters, and especially those of the villages, are adept at producing both utilitarian wares and figures of gods and goddesses for the annual cycle of festivals and religious ceremonies. Some have become highly respected and famed for their striking interpretation of local deities, folk heroes and the animals and mythical creatures of ritual. As ever in so complex a culture as India's, there are exceptions to this rule, and some potters do specialize in making idols, mostly for the densely populated urban centres. Of these, the best known are the effigy makers of the states of West Bengal and Bihar in eastern India, and of Calcutta in particular, who have become organized into communities of specialist craftsmen. For these potters, their daily routine is associated with the manufacture of small clay or plaster sculptures of the popular deities, especially Durga, Kali, Lakshmi and Saraswati. Larger commissions are also undertaken, including eight-metre-high images with a body of wood and straw covered with a skin of clay, all essential items in the frantic celebrations with which a panoply of gods and goddesses are worshipped each festival season.

To begin to comprehend just what fervour can be generated by the preparations for an urban festival in India, there can be few more eye-opening experiences than a visit to Calcutta during the weeks before Dussehra. Held in late September or October when the monsoon season is on its way out, this ten-day festival commemorates Durga's victory over Mahisha, the fierce buffalo demon. Each community, neighbourhood and district of the city and its suburbs applies itself to the presentation of this epic scene by building temporary temples complete with brightly painted and dressed models. To supply such a demand, whole sections of the city are devoted to their manufacture.

A visit to the effigy makers' quarter at first reveals little sign of the scale of this work. Fearful of a drenching from the last of the monsoon downpours, the craftsmen hide their figures in their workshops, and to discover the secret stores within it is necessary to be bold and inquisitive. Ushered into the damp gloom by a surprised and delighted artist, one begins to discern the shapes of arms, hands and heads, many painted with fearsome expressions made all the more sinister by a coat of glistening varnish; others, in an unfinished state, have the serene gaze of a Greek statue. The scale of manufacture is quite extraordinary, for each stall and workshop holds hundreds of deities of all sizes, from benches packed with life-size mannequins to shelves laden with small clay sculptures and vividly painted plaster casts.

Rambling happily from one group of figures to another, one may be taken in hand by a willing assistant and guided to nearby workshops devoted to the making of the larger straw images. Binding bundles of straw together, tying limbs into position and wrestling with headless torsos, the men and boys constructed the core of these deities with alacrity and great good humour, so that in minutes an upright stanchion of wood is transformed into the well padded and proportioned figure of a goddess. Not surprisingly, the stage of construction that follows, the application of a clay outer skin, is much enjoyed by the younger apprentices and boys. Their slapping on and smoothing of handfuls of glutinous clay is also accompanied by much mirth, for it is not every youth who enjoys the opportunity to mould a deity; and until the final ceremonial stage when the eyes are painted on to the face the effigy possesses no supernatural powers.

The village potter also has his religious duties and privileges, as befits his age-old role in the creation of objects from the earth itself. The potter is blessed with the divine endowment of creativity, and the wheel and kiln are venerated as the gifts of the god. At a marriage ceremony the potter's wheel is worshipped in the ritual of *chak puja* as a representation of the constant movement of the cosmos. In many central and southern communities the potter is granted priestly duties, especially associated with the creation, installation and maintenance of terracotta icons.

Some forty kilometres north of Udaipur in southern Rajasthan is the village of Molela, home to a potter community well known for the sculpting of relief plaques depicting Hindu gods and local Rajput heroes. Until recently the principal buyers of these plaques were the tribal and village people of the Mewar region, such as the Gujar, Meena, Garasia and Katara. Preparing for the harvest festival season of January and February, the Molela potter produces thousands of protective idols of beings such as Dharmaraj, Ganeshji, Bhairava and the Mother Goddess as Durga, as well as the local neo-Vaishnava heroes, now the accepted deities of Dev Narayan and Pabuji. Made of clay mixed with donkey dung, the plaques are often decorated with particularly bright and shining colours, mixed with gum from local trees to make it adhere well to the clay. The final lustre is achieved by coating the surface with *jala*, a mixture of ghee and linseed oil. Sold at the massive fairs and festivals particular to each region, and for which Rajasthan and Gujarat are famous, or collected directly from the workshop by groups of tribal people, these plaques are installed in village shrines with much rejoicing, feasting and prayer.

There is a widespread ritual of offering sculptured clay animals to appease a local god, to thank him for a favour or to goad

THE MAKING OF A CLAY VOTIVE PLAQUE

Not far from the temple town of Nathdwara in southern Rajasthan lies the village of Molela. The workshops of the potters are dominated by the successful tradition of making votive plaques of both local as well as more widely worshipped deities and heroes. Squatting on the mud floor, the potter begins his task by rolling out and cutting a prepared clay backdrop (above and right) for the deity.

Working quickly, scraps of
glutinous clay are finger-rolled
and cut to shape with a wooden
blade before being pressed onto
the plinth and smoothed into
place as canopy decoration.
Another wafer-thin slab of clay is
then pressed into position (right)
and lifted from the centre into a
hollow dome to form the head and
body of the benevolent elephant
god, Ganesh.

The work progresses in stages
and once the body has been
formed it is left to harden before
the application of decorations and
auspicious motifs. Taking stone
and clay dies from a bowl by his
side, the potter makes a series of
stamped rosettes that are then
moistened and pressed onto the
evolving effigy (above right). For
the crown, a wooden knife is used
to incise a fan of clay (above)
and two coils of clay are twisted
together to form a forehead
decoration. It is now ready for
drying and firing (right).

Elsewhere in the workshop the
potter's assistants prepare other
deities, which after being dried in
the shade for a week will be given
a pre-kiln bake in the hot sun.
After amassing some fifty
plaques, an open-air kiln is built,
fired by cow cakes and thorn-bush
wood. The baked terracottas later
emerge from the ashes with an
orange finish. Many are sold for
use as village deities; others are
painted with startlingly bright
colours mixed with vegetable gum
and given a final glaze of a
mixture of butter and linseed oil.

him into action. In Uttar Pradesh, in the Gorakhpur and Azamgarh areas, there is a tradition among the local potters of sculpting these votive figures. Elephants and horses are their most popular work, decorated with an ornate appliqué of clay whorls, diamonds, stripes and waves, made even more effective by a fringe of clay bells, and a gleaming finish to the unpainted terracotta. The Bhil tribes of Chhota Udaipur in Gujarat and adjacent Jhabua in Madhya Pradesh place their trust in such animal offerings; their potters mould distinctive clay horses, camels, elephants, tigers and bullocks that are then offered to a village deity, or to a revered animal itself such as the tiger. Set down in the sacred grove that always lies in a secluded spot near the settlement, the terracotta animals are clustered together in a jumble of new and old, all eventually disintegrating and returning to the earth in their turn.

In Darbhanga, Bihar, the offering of gaily painted terracotta horses and riders, elephants, handmaidens and lions is another example of the presentation of sculptures in thanks for the answering of a prayer. In Darbhanga, however, these effigies are not hidden away in a quiet glade, but placed for worship in a courtyard or by a shrine, if possible under a tree. There are two separate categories of shrine in honour of these local deities or *gramadevata*. One serves the higher castes in their worship of Ghorkalesh, a Brahman youth who died unmarried and whose soul wanders the earth. To give the soul a refuge and home, the horse is offered, acting as a vehicle for the youth in his role as protector of the community from evil. For the Dusadhs, a less well born community of the district, the horse and rider is offered to Sailesh, their own mythical and protective hero from the foothills of the Himalayas.

Of all the effigies to the protective gods of the villages of India, the terracotta sculptures of the south dedicated to the Lord Aiyanar, son of Vishnu, the Preserver, and Shiva, the Creator and Destroyer, are the most dramatic. The sanctuary to Aiyanar is often found in a grove on the banks of a pond, and his representation may vary from an undecorated stone slab set standing under a tree to an ornately sculpted and brightly painted terracotta rider set confidently astride a horse or elephant. Driving along a rutted track between the many and densely arrayed villages and hamlets of Tamil Nadu, one may be seized with amazement at the sight of such a place. It is not so much the statue of the god himself that is so striking, but that of his horses or *kudirai*. Rearing high up into the sky, seemingly above the glade of trees, these magnificent terracotta horses, as much as six metres high and clustered in rows or chaotic herds of many score and more, represent steeds for Aiyanar and his companions, so that he may complete his nightly protective ride around the village.

HORSE AND RIDER EFFIGIES OF BIHAR

As the mount of the Aryan invaders, the horse is revered with a sense of awe by many of the rural peoples of India. In the Darbhanga district of Bihar, brightly painted horse and rider effigies are seen by temples and at shrines under trees, acting as warrior guards (below). The same coiling and hand-moulding processes (opposite) are used by the potters of the area for purely decorative artefacts as well (left).

This throng of horses reveals the extent of the struggle enacted after each sunset, for Aiyanar is always supported by a host of heroes, the *vira*, who oppose his devilish companion and shadow Karuppan, riding alongside with his own entourage of demons in the never ending struggle between good and evil.

Unlike potters elsewhere in India, the makers of these horses, the *kusavan*, are accorded an elevated status, tracing an ancestry to the union between a Brahman and a Harijan woman. Commissioned on an auspicious day to replace one or more of the ever decaying effigies made by his predecessors, the potter is assisted by his wife and children in the making of the components for these expressive figures. For all but the very largest horses, the legs are made of tubes of rolled clay and the body is built up to the neck in stages by coiling the clay. The head is applied last, and then the whole assembly is sun-dried. The clay trimmings for the sculpture often consist of bells, mirrors, crocodiles, splayed figures and grotesque faces, and these are formed separately before being applied to the neck, head and flanks of the horse. Such trappings as the mirrors and bells are said to warn the evil-doers of the imminent approach of Aiyanar, while the grotesque faces and crocodiles are intended to strike terror in their hearts.

The baking of the sculpture takes place in an open kiln, fuelled by straw and cow-dung cakes and insulated with old pots and mud. Large sculptures, such as the giant horses, are made in component parts, fired, assembled and fired again. Painted decoration is commonplace and such daubing adds further character to the assembly: the faces and heads are often coloured red to depict anger, and the necks and bodies are often a deep blue, denoting calm. The commissioning of a new sculpture is a cause for great celebration and the terracotta is carried shoulder-high to the sacred grove at a propitious moment, amid much noise and gaiety. When it is set in place, life is given to the figure through the painting of the eyes by the potter. The occasion may be marked by animal sacrifice, a practice shunned by Brahman priests, so the potter himself acts as *pujari* or priest, leading the throng in worship.

Styles of decoration and expression in the Aiyanar sculptures have become standardized in recent decades. The sculptures that fill the numerous temple groves scattered throughout Pudukottai and Salem districts of Tamil Nadu illustrate a regional fashion for a reduction in dimensions and an over-zealous use of facial features. Aside from the giant concrete-reinforced stucco horses, which are more akin to gaily painted fairground steeds, the making of the towering terracotta horses now seems to be a craft of the past with many potters now making horses and riders for a national and international gallery marketplace.

AIYANAR SHRINES OF TAMIL NADU

Often hidden within groves of trees, or set beside the highway and thus visible for miles, are the temples dedicated to Aiyanar and his associated deities: warriors, horses and oxen. Magnificent chargers (previous page left) are made and fired in situ; smaller examples are made in the compound of the potter priest (previous page right).

A MISCELLANY OF CRAFTS

BASKETS TO PUPPETS

Benefiting from the increasing number of travellers who visit India each year and supplying the recent demand from the indigenous urban market, the craftsmen and women of certain communities in India are flourishing. The brightly coloured grass baskets (left) of Mithila, Bihar, and the puppets of Jodhpur in Rajasthan (above) are now sold far and wide.

The visitor to India cannot fail to be excited and often bewildered by the array of traditional arts and crafts on offer in the bazaars of every town and city, as well as in the trinket and curio shops of hotels and tourist centres. Some of these artefacts, such as the papier-mâché boxes of Kashmir and of Jaipur in Rajasthan, have been made for the European and tourist market for many decades. This work has therefore become highly stylized, and has also been made more appealing to the buyer by using relatively costly materials such as real gold or silver paint, and by adding intricate decoration. By contrast, some of the arts and crafts of the Indian villages, and particularly the performing arts, are becoming ever more difficult to find. In recent years the traditional making of puppets and masks and their use in performance has declined in popularity. Yet it is well worth the effort to seek out the wonderfully energetic entertainment afforded by mask or puppet plays in such states as Bihar, Kerala and Rajasthan. More universal in every way is the everyday use of baskets and mats throughout India. One cannot help but be struck by the tremendous variation in the sizes and shapes of the baskets, their simple elegance concealing the perfect match of function with design.

SIMPLE BASKETS OF UTILITY

Across the length and breadth of India baskets are woven from local raw materials to shapes and dimensions that admirably match the lifestyles of their owners.

These fisherwomen (right) of Rameshwaram in Tamil Nadu float their capacious bamboo baskets by their sides on planks of wood, ready for the catch.

FODDER AND PACK BASKETS

For this farmer at the Nagaur fair in Rajasthan, a basket of reeds from a nearby river proves a fine feeding trough for his beloved cows (left). In the high lands of Ladakh, the haulage of goods up and down the precipitous slopes is made easier

by the use of strong willow baskets. Robust, yet pliable, willow is harvested from the riverbanks and such back-borne baskets (far right) will carry everything from children to produce destined for sale at the local market.

THE BASKET AND MAT WEAVER

For more than a thousand years the simplest crafts of India have been considered lowly occupations. The ancient and elegant craft of working vegetable fibres into useful and decorative baskets and mats is one such calling, along with those of making pots and weaving cloth. Served by an abundant source of materials, needing almost no tools, and quite without arcane technical secrets, basketry and mat weaving share with pottery the distinction of being the earliest human crafts. The earliest archaeological evidence for this fact, found in north-west India, links the two crafts with the finding of an ancient pot bearing the imprint of a fibre mat.

As a craft of the indigenous inhabitants of the subcontinent, and especially those forest dwellers now known as the *adivasis*, or 'tribals', basket and mat making are described dismissively by the Aryan scriptures, which go as far as to designate a life of such work as a suitable punishment for one of their errant kings. Today, the best of the craft continues to be associated with, and largely practised by, the peoples of the south. The role of these craftsmen remains an essential part of the Indian economy in spite of rapid technological change. The basket weavers supply cheap, durable and environmentally sound containers for the carriage of essential goods throughout India. Whether they bear the produce of the farmer, the rubble of the building worker, coal from the ground or fish from the ocean, these baskets are, as ever, objects of essential use and simple beauty.

India offers diverse materials for the weaving, twining and coiling of baskets and mats. In the mountainous north the wild and cultivated willow are the predominant staples for the basket craftsmen. The Kashmir Valley is renowned for its farmed plantations of lakeside willow, introduced by the British in the nineteenth century, when a basket-making institute was also set up to train young men in the craft. Objects suited to Western tastes – simple, undecorated hampers, garden chairs, lampshades and trays – as well as baskets of a more indigenous kind continue to be the mainstay of their production. This is centred at Lake Nagin in Srinagar, and has spread throughout the quarter adjacent to the Hazratbal mosque. More local in origin, however, is the making of the body warmer known as a *kangri*. This is the essential accessory for every Kashmiri in winter, and comprises a small wild willow basket with a carrying handle, in which an earthenware pot containing hot coals is set. Carried underneath a shawl or gown, the device is a means of alleviating the bitter cold of this mountainous region.

To the east of Kashmir the people of the high desert kingdom of Ladakh rely on the strength and capaciousness of their own designs of backpack baskets, in which they carry all manner of goods up and down the steep slopes. Made of a local strain of riverside willow or of reed, known as *malchang* and *chipkiang* respectively, the conical, flat-bottomed willow baskets are essential equipment for every family. Slung across the back and secured with a woven rope of goat hair, the wide-mouthed panniers are perfect for carrying children, chickens, fuel and foodstuffs. For carrying vegetables to the market the *tsepo* basket is used; a larger version for hauling fodder is known as a *phukstel*. More versatile is the finer reed, which when soaked forms a soft strand that is woven by the men into a variety of pack baskets as well as the floor matting known as *shakstar*.

Descending from the Himalayas, the use of bamboo and cane becomes predominant in the construction of baskets and similar goods. In order to create a usable strand from these tough plants, the stems of bamboo and cane are cut into the necessary lengths and then split with a machete. If necessary these strips may then be softened by soaking in water or bending over the flame of a lamp. The tribal peoples of the north-eastern states, especially Tripura and Manipur, manage their groves of bamboo as a crop, supplying the soaring poles which are used to build houses and bridges but which, when split and woven, become baskets, mats, umbrellas, awnings, screens, fish traps, winnowing trays and sun-shielding hats.

West of Calcutta, in the district of Midnapur, the weavers of floor mats are famous for their fine work, which is in demand throughout the region. Such mats are densely woven from the finely split marsh reeds called *mutra*. After harvesting these reeds are stored in a pond before being boiled in water, when they take on colours from creamy white to beige and brown. A more brazen colouring is obtained by dyeing the reeds before weaving. The stems are sorted into bundles of uniform thickness, then stiffened with rice starch before being woven into mats of a soothing hue and texture by women working in pairs on the simplest of ground looms. They excel in creating a variety of figurative and floral motifs. Just as the work of these village women is popular in the nearby city of Calcutta, so the weaver of the tall *sarkanda* grass in Uttar Pradesh and Haryana finds a ready market for his furnishing wares in the metropolis of Delhi. It is a common sight to find this type of craftsman at work by the side of a country road, his completed stools and chairs made of latticed grass with a wheat-straw and cloth binding ready for sale by his side.

Beyond the Deccan, land of the tribes who weave a tremendous variety of traditional baskets for their everyday needs,

BASKETS FROM MITHILA, BIHAR

Not only do these craftsmen and women construct colourful storage baskets and boxes from the local grass known as sikki *(below), but there is also a thriving production of the popular two-dimensional figures that represent well known Hindu deities such as* Ganesh *(left). Equally colourful are the bamboo baskets for everyday use (opposite), patterned with highly fugitive dyes.*

MAT AND SCREEN WEAVING

Lowland West Bengal is characterized by its lush green paddy fields and palm groves. In such a climate the waterways are rich with grasses ideal for the weaving of fine floor mats. Beyond Midnapore a mother and daughter practise the craft of madur grass weaving in the shaded cool of their verandah (left). Highly prized in Calcutta, these mats often have warps of jute fibres.

In the south, which is subject to the bi-annual vagaries of the monsoon, it is as well to live in easily repairable homes. Woven bamboo screens (opposite) provide ideal room dividers for the peoples of Tamil Nadu.

lie the palm-dotted paddies and hillsides thicketed with bamboo that make up the landscape of Tamil Nadu and Kerala. Here in the south, the coconut, date and palmyra palms contribute their fibres to the range of baskets and mats; a tremendous variety of local plants is also employed, including the screw-pine, bamboo, cane, grasses and reeds. Not only are domestic utensils made of these fibres, but the architecture of the south is dominated by their use. Outside the towns and cities, homes are made of mud or brick walls capped by a grass or leaf thatch, a cost-free, easily repaired roof in a land frequently struck by tropical squalls during the twice-yearly monsoon of this region.

Bamboo is the principal material for the everyday carrying baskets of the town and countryside alike; when these are used to store or carry food grains the weave is often given an impervious coating of cow manure that soon dries in the hot sun. For the strongest baskets, used for hauling building rubble, sand and mud, the stem of the forest plant known as *azhingi* is used. The leaves of the date palm are harvested for the weaving of baskets, and palmyra leaves and fibres are braided into ropes, mats and screens. More attractive to the urban market are the brightly dyed palmyra leaves that are woven and ingeniously intertwined into an extensive range of forms such as picnic and shopping baskets, table mats and coasters, hand fans, trinket

caskets, handbags, baby's rattles, and toy animals and birds. Rameshwaram in Tamil Nadu is well known for this imaginative and functional woven work.

As might be imagined, the basket weaving of the south extends to the manufacture of a great variety of floor mats as well. The coarsest examples, woven from materials such as screw pine and palmyra leaf, may be turned out at the rate of two or three a day by an experienced weaver; but the nationally famous *korai* grass rugs, made of fibres sliced as fine as the hair of a buffalo, may take more than three weeks. Pathamadai village in Thirunelveli district, Tamil Nadu, is known for its production of the finest *korai* mats, a craft practised by women, who interlace the grass wefts through the cotton or silk warps with a wooden needle. Once always coloured with vegetable dyes, these mats are now found in a natural grass finish or patterned with bands of the brightest synthetic tones such as fluorescent orange and startling purple. Mats of a coarse texture, by contrast, are woven in Kerala and Tamil Nadu from the sword-shaped thorny leaves of a succulent shrub known as screw-pine. Most are constructed in a simple twill weave, seen as the weft passing over two warp elements, and legend tells of the Keralan seafarers using such mats as sails. The craft has been much encouraged by government agencies resulting in new forms, such as tablemats.

THE MAKER OF PAPIER-MÂCHÉ

Papier mâché, a craft for which Kashmir is renowned, is thought to have been introduced from Central Asia by the Muslims before the Mughal era. Then, as now, the technique of constructing an object, or the *sakhtasazi* process, and its painting, known as *naqashi*, are two quite separate tasks; both are laborious. The first involves the kneading of soaked waste paper, cloth, rice straw and copper sulphate into a pulp which is then pressed around a mould made of clay, wood or metal. When the pulp is dry the shape is cut away from the mould in two halves with a fine saw and glued together again. The surface is coated with a white layer of gypsum and glue, rubbed smooth with a stone or baked piece of clay, and pasted with layers of tissue paper to prevent the substrate from cracking. Finally the object is sandpapered and burnished, ready for the colourful artistry of the *naqash* or painter, who seals his work with several coats of a varnish made of linseed oil and pine resin.

This was an art form beloved of the Mughals, and under their rule the Kashmiri craftsmen were commissioned to mould and paint all manner of furniture and architectural fittings, including doors, window frames, shutters, wall and ceiling panels, and even bed frames. During the seventeenth century early European travellers discovered this highly decorative and marketable craft, and from that time on the papier-mâché artists of Kashmir tailored some of their production to the needs of a foreign trade that demanded nested boxes, vases and other suitably exotic trinkets. In common with the Kashmiri shawl trade, the business boomed. Since the late nineteenth century the tourist and export market has dominated the craft, with the result that simpler, smaller and cheaper artefacts such as trays, caddies and picture frames are produced in great quantity without the quality and decorative zeal of the past.

Workshops, or *karkhana*, of excellence still exist where more traditional forms such as the larger jewellery boxes are moulded and painted for a wealthier, more discerning clientele. For this market sumptuous decorations of gold leaf, as well as pure gold and silver paint, are used to splendidly ostentatious effect. The application of gold leaf is a delicate task. The areas to receive the precious metal are painted with a warm solution of glue and sugar, and the fine sheets of gold are laid on the surface, bonding only to the prepared pattern. An embossed effect is achieved by a similar technique of brushing on a solution of adhesive; here the raised pattern is created by the application of layers of gypsum and glue which, when set, are highlighted with paint.

PAPIER MÂCHÉ OF RAJASTHAN AND KASHMIR

When imprisoned in the magnificent Central Asian city of Samarkand some 500 years ago, a young Kashmiri prince observed his captors' predilection for the craft of using paper pulp as the base for painted and lacquered artefacts. By combining Kashmiri talents in the execution of delicate line and colour with this simple new material, a world renowned craft was established. The first articles produced were rectangular pen-and-brush boxes, known as kalamdans, *literally pen case work. The Mughals displayed a voracious delight and desire for the papier mâché of Kashmir, often commissioning entire communities and workshops to produce boxes, palace decorations and furniture to their sumptuous specifications.*

Emulating the exquisite work and traditional styles of their ancestors, the naqash *master craftsmen of today copy in intricate detail such scenes as the Mughal court in session, or the nobility at the hunt, and also continue to borrow patterns from Kashmir shawls, the most popular of which is a highly stylized tree of life. The accurate representation of individual flowers such as the water lily, field crocus and narcissus is an enduringly popular subject, as are the floral motifs in the* hazzara *or 'thousand flowers' composition depicting in a dense and colourful haze all the blooms found in the Kashmir Valley.*

RAJASTHANI PUPPETS

Carving and chiselling with deft alacrity, blocks of mango wood (top) are transformed into the heads of the puppet heroes and villains of the Rajput epic, Amar Singh Rathor. The puppets are identified by their facial characteristics (above) as well as their costumes (right). Legend tells of the first puppeteer, or nat, being created by Brahma to amuse and beguile his wife Saraswati. So successful was this entertainment and the resultant intrigues, that the puppeteer was banished to earth. In Rajasthan it is the caste of nat bhats who entertain the villagers with their puppeteering, music and juggling (opposite).

THE PUPPET MAKER

Throughout Asia, for thousands of years, the puppet theatre has been not only a favourite entertainment but a means of preserving regional folklore, myths and legends. In India its popular role has now largely been supplanted by television; another factor in its decline has been more widespread literacy among rural and urban populations alike. Yet so pervasive and familiar are the stories, taken most commonly from the beloved Ramayana and Mahabharata epics, that the puppeteer of India continues to survive and practise his art, although in dwindling numbers and mostly among the poorer communities, especially those of the south.

Many varieties of puppetry once flourished in India; from the evidence of their appearance in the very first book of the Mahabharata, it seems that they were widespread as early as the ninth century BC. Today the centres of this art are more thinly scattered. In the north the gaily painted and dressed string marionettes, or *kathputalis*, are found in Rajasthan; and large dolls known as *putul nauch*, made of clay and rice husks modelled on a rod, are a traditional form in West Bengal. In the latter, stories from the Mahabharata epic and that of the snake goddess Manasa Devi are performed. The lack of mobility inherent in the design of the dolls is more than made up for by the lively action of the puppeteer. The animated shadow puppet shows of the Deccan and southern India were originally created as a means of entertaining the temple deities.

The string-operated *kathputalis* of Rajasthan stylishly depict medieval Rajput heroes. A turban, headdress or shawl of cloth sprinkled with glitter crowns a wooden head painted with prominent eyes and a white or yellow complexion; the male figures are completed by a spectacular moustache and beard. The torso is an extension of the wooden head and supports rag-stuffed arms; legs and feet are not necessary, as most of the dolls are dressed in the full skirt or dress of brightly patterned material which was the regional costume of the period. Such a garb emphasizes the vigorous whirls and jumps of the characters. The folk play, Amar Singh Rathor, is primarily enacted for entertainment, giving great scope for amusing trick puppetry. What moral instruction exists is exemplified by the heroic actions of the characters, enhanced by the songs and narration of the performers. Latterly, these puppeteers have become more renowned for their selling of the colourful dolls and their exhibition performances in tourist hotels than as purveyors of historical and amusing tales to the rural communities.

The shadow plays of the central and southern states, in contrast, have roots in an altogether more richly creative tradition of religious observance and instruction. They are necessarily enacted at night, and the shadows cast by the puppets on to a cloth screen create a sense of mystery, awe and divine inspiration in the audience as they watch with devotion the unfolding of the epic. Near Palghat, in Kerala, there are some eight families who continue to make and use shadow puppets known as *tolpava koothu*, from *tol* meaning leather, *pava*, puppet, and *koothu*, story.

Central to the annual cycle of performances that takes place during the dry season is the complete rendering of the Ramayana, adapted and divided into twenty-one parts for the shadow puppet theatre, and presented over twenty-one consecutive nights. Such a marathon is commissioned by the dominant local temple dedicated to the goddess Kali who, it is believed, will be watching the whole show with pleasure and gratitude.

Over 130 puppets are needed for the presentation of the Ramayana. Because the theatre performs within a temple sanctuary, the puppets have always been made of deerskin, owing to this animal's sacred associations. In the performance there are numerous occasions, such as battle scenes, when characters are literally thrown against each other for a most dramatic interplay of shadows; not surprisingly, some of the most bellicose puppets have a short life. Taking such a battered hero or villain, the puppeteer copies its outline on a prepared skin and then uses a variety of coarse and fine chisels to cut away the leather, faithfully reproducing the facial expression, decorations and stance of the original. As a support to the thin leather and as a central handle for the performer, a split bamboo stick is sewn the length of the puppet. The finished assembly is painted: although this is invisible to the audience, the colouring allows the puppeteer to recognize and reach for a character instantly during the fast-moving action of some of the scenes.

The most important characters are represented in the three different postures of sitting, walking and fighting, by three separate puppets. The seated conversationalists and walking characters gesture to emphasize the story with one arm, but those engaged in combat have two movable arms with which they can brandish their weapons. The action is supplemented by a host of secondary puppets depicting beasts and birds, as well as by the backdrops to the epic, such as trees, lakes and mountains.

The shadow puppet playhouse, or *koothu madam*, is a low purpose-built structure, positioned to face the goddess Kali in the adjacent temple. Opening on to a bare earth amphitheatre, the stage is fronted with a twelve-metre-long thin white cotton cloth, below which runs an opaque cloth in black which hides the movements of the puppeteers. A central horizontal wooden beam serves as the platform for the lighting, which comes from the flames of twenty-one coconut-oil lamps set in their own half shells. The puppets are offered up above the black curtain, their shadows brought to life by the flickering lamps and the puppeteers' dexterous manipulation of the rods and arms. Combined with the sometimes frenzied pace of the rhythmical sing-song dialogue and the clamour of the drum and cymbals, the scenes from the Ramayana create a mixture of excitement and childlike wonder, as the gods battle against the agents of evil.

KERALA SHADOW PUPPETS

Surrounded by old and new examples of hide shadow puppets, this puppeteer (opposite) is also responsible for the replication of worn-out puppets. When held up to the backlit cloth screen during an evening performance these characters from the Ramayana epic come alive (below). Before every show the god Ganesh is offered to the audience (left).

Kerala is also the home of a glove puppet theatre known as *pavakathakali*. Centred on Palghat district, this is a puppet imitation of the well known Keralan *kathakali* classical dance and theatre; this form of mimicry is thought to have been adopted by the existing local tradition of puppet plays during the eighteenth century. In decline until recently, *pavakathakali* has energetically been revived, along with other lesser known puppet traditions.

THE MAKER OF MASKS

Long practised by the independent tribal peoples of India, the wearing of masks for the primitive ceremonies of fertility, initiation and spirit possession is a ritual act that has been zealously preserved in the private world of their forest and jungle homes. Yet the inevitable spread of the Hindu peoples and the growing intrusion of modern life are causing scores of these observances to disappear every year.

In many districts of Bihar, West Bengal and Orissa, however, there exists a flourishing culture of masked dancing. A popular entertainment during the spring festivals dedicated to Nata Bhairava, the frightening dance incarnation of Shiva, as well as to the deity Ardhanarishvara, who represents Shiva and Shakti joined together in one form, the spectacle is staged by dancers wearing painted clay or papier-mâché masks known as *chhau*. These masks depict not only the recognizable characters of the Hindu epics – demons, heroes, animals, birds, deities and court dancers – but also their emotions. This is achieved by the fine painting of stylized expressions on the masks, which are coloured with a background of subdued pastel shades. The actors in their *chhau* masks and expressive costumes dance the roles of their characters with a possessed frenzy.

One of the most popular of the masked plays of northern India, however, occurs in *raslila* theatre. Staged for the members of the Vaishnava cult, the plays expound on the life of Krishna. Masks are used to heighten the spectacle by portraying not only the faces of gods and goddesses, but also the expressions of the mortals. Mathura is a major centre for the production of such masks, which may be most elaborately decorated with *zari* or gold-thread work, emphasizing the devilish ferocity of characters such as the ten-headed Ravana. The plays are not mere entertainments but move the audience to an ecstasy of reverence for the god; as ever in this land where every part of life is pervaded by religion, and many an act is one of devotion.

GLOVE PUPPETS AND MASKS

The district of Palghat in Kerala is known for the traditional puppet plays known as pavakathakali, in which wooden-headed glove puppets, some 300 to 600 cm tall, enact episodes from the Mahabharata. Dressed and painted in the style of kathakali dancers, the figure of Bhima adorns his beloved wife Panchali with flowers (opposite left) and Shiva is seen with his consort Parvati (opposite right).

Chhau masked dancing is practised in West Bengal, Bihar and Orissa, and depicts the victory of good over evil. The masks portray all manner of demons and men (above and left).

GLOSSARY

Aarathi: for home or temple use, the hand-held small votive lamps which often have a carved handle in animal form. Often found in the temple sanctuaries of Tamil Nadu.

Agasala: silver- and goldsmiths.

Ajrakh: blue and red cloth of Gujarat and Rajasthan; the name is thought to be derived from the Arabic word for blue, *azrak*. These cloths are block-printed in a complicated sequence of resist and mordant resist techniques.

Alpona: floor paintings of Bengal.

Anchal: Bengali name for a *pallav* or *muhun*, the decorated end section of a sari.

Andaa: pot for water storage.

Angula: unit of measurement for a sculptor. A *hasta* is made up of 24 *angulas*.

Aripana: floor paintings of Bihar.

Aripona: floor paintings of other regions of northern India.

Ayurvedic: scriptures of medicine.

Azhingi: the stem of the forest plant used to make baskets.

Bagh: lit. 'garden'. A form of Punjabi dowry needlework.

Bandhani: tie-and-dye cloth.

Bhakti: the worship of the image of a god.

Bhanvatiya: nose ring and disc of metal, often supported by a chain to the ear.

Bharatias: brass craftsmen.

Bhatti: a potter's kiln.

Bhogi pandigai: the day before **Pongal.**

Bhopas: wandering bards.

Bidri: decorated metalwork named after the town of Bidar in north-eastern Karnataka.

Brihatsamhitha: an early 6th-century treatise on astronomy by Varahamihira.

Bukani: silver powder composed of lead, zinc and mercury.

Butidar: brocaded cloth, often with floral motifs (*butis*).

Cauk (or *chowk*): home to the goddess Palghat in Warli paintings; also town square.

Chaitya: shrine.

Chak puja: prayers before a potter's wheel; part of marriage ceremony.

Chak: potter's wheel.

Chakla: embroidered, appliqué or patchwork square panels.

Chapati: unleavened bread.

Chatera: engraver.

Chay: madder.

Chhau: painted masks of clay or papier mâché.

Chikri: a wood with the qualities of ivory, being light in colour and possessing little grain.

Chipkiang: reed of Ladakh.

Chippa: cloth printing and dyeing community.

Chitrakatha: the narrative scrolls of the wandering bards.

Choli: blouse.

Choolah: stove.

Churru: water pot.

Chutti paanai: cooking vessel for pulses.

Deepalakshmi: a lamp, in the form of a female statue carrying oil.

Deepam: lamp.

Dhokra: lost wax work of the tribal craftsmen.

Dhow: Arab trading vessel.

Dhurrie: cotton flat weave.

Dhyana: meditation.

Diwali: the festival of lamps.

Dravidian: linguistic group of the south.

Dudhi: white wood.

Dupatta: shawl worn by women.

Gadia lohars: lit. 'cart [itinerant] blacksmiths'.

Gaghra: skirt.

Gangaalam: pot for water storage.

Gara: a system of barter for the village potter; in Ladakhi, 'a blacksmith'.

Ghara: water pot.

Ghat: riverbank steps.

Golusu: anklets, in solid bands or chains.

Gopurams: towers of a temple.

Hamsa besari: gem-covered gold ornament in the shape of a swan, piercing the nose.

Hamsa: mythical swan.

Hansli: choker worn by men as well as women.

Harijan: low-caste community renamed by Gandhi; lit. 'children of god'.

Hari nila: the colour of water in which the sky is reflected.

Hasta: unit of measurement for a sculptor; the length from elbow to the tip of the middle finger.

Haveli: merchant's mansion.

Hazara: lit. 'thousand flowers'; form of decorative composition.

Howdah: pavilion or seat strapped on to an elephant's back.

Ikat: tied-and-dyed woven cloth, from the Malay word *mengikat*, meaning to tie or bind.

Indigo: blue dye (*Indigofera tinctoria*).

Jaggery: palm sugar.

Jala: a solution of ghee and linseed oil.

Jali: latticework in stone or wood.

Jamdani: fine patterned cotton.

Jaria: setter of stones; also *kundansaz*.

Jhumkas: dangling earrings.

Jimikki: bell-shaped ear drops of gold and stones.

Joshi: a clan of the *chippa* textile printing community.

Jyonti: wall painting of Uttar Pradesh.

Kada: a series of wide bracelets for the wrists and arms.

Kadi: anklet.

Kal-tac'chan: stonemason.

Kalamkari: lit. 'pen work'; textile with designs and colours executed by pen.

Kammalan: a group of five high-caste artisans.

Kandhani: girdle.

Kangri: Kashmiri personal warmer. A willow basket containing an earthenware pot of hot coals.

Kankanam: a rack of bangles.

Kantha: embroidered cloth of Bengal.

Karhai: large cooking vessel. Also, *patila*.

Karkhana: workshop.

Karvad: portable temple.

Kashi: 'city of light'. Benares (Varanasi).

Kathi: farming community of Gujarat.

Kathakali: dance theatre of Kerala.

Kathputalis: string puppets of Rajasthan.

Khadi: hand spun and woven cotton cloth.

Kharal: large mortar.

Khatumband: intricate geometrically-patterned woodwork of Kashmir.

Khotri: dowry bag.

Kinkhab: gold brocaded cloth.

Kolam: southern floor paintings.

Koothu madam: shadow puppet playhouse.

Korai: fine grass-woven mats.

Kovara: potter in Kanarese.

Kudam: pot for carrying water, shaped to rest against the hip.

Kudirai: horses of Aiyanar.

Kumbhar: potter. The Sanskrit prefix *ku* means 'of the earth' and a clay pitcher is a known as a *kumbha*. Also, *kumbhakara* and *kumar*.

Kummara: potter in Telegu.

Kundan: Mughal-inspired setting of stones, whereby gems are framed with gold leaf.

Kundansaz: setter of stones, also *jaria*.

Kusavan: maker of effigies. Tamil Nadu and Malayalam.

Kuthu-vilakku: a five-wicked free standing lamp of brass.

Laheria: cloth with striped patterning. Lit. 'waves'.

Lingam: phallic symbol of Shiva.

Lohar: blacksmith.

Lota: personal water vessel.

Lungi: man's unstitched lower garment wrap.

Maatu pongal: pongal for cows. The day after Pongal.

Mahabharatha: Hindu epic.

Malchang: riverside willow, often made into baskets. Ladakh.

Malwias: itinerant blacksmiths and wood carvers.

Mandana: auspicious paintings of Rajasthan.

Mangalasuthra: marriage talisman. Also, *thaali*.

Marwaris: merchant and banking community of Rajasthan.

Mashru: mixed cloth of silk and cotton. Gujarat.

Mata ni pachedi: painted and printed cloth panel, made by the Vaghri community of Ahmedabad.

Mata no chandarvo: painted and printed cloth shrine canopies made by the Vaghri community of Ahmedabad.

Meenakar: the enameller.

Meenakari: champlevé enamelling process.

Meghwal: caste of leather workers.

Metti: toe ring.

Mistri: carpentry and carving community.

Mochi: professional embroiderers.

Mohalla: dwelling quarter of a settlement.

Mor: peacock.

Mordant: a substance used to fix dye colour.

Muhun: the decorated endpiece of a sari and *dupatta* (shawl). Also, *pallav* or *anchal.*

Muslin: fine woven cotton.

Mutra: marsh reeds.

Naagar: hair decorations to the back of the head, usually a five-headed serpent in gold.

Nali: finger ring.

Naqash: painter of papier mâché.

Naqashi: incised floral patterns.

Nat bhats: wandering entertainers.

Nath: small jewelled or silver nose stud. Also, *nathu.*

Nauratna: ring, or equivalent necklace, set with the nine stones linked with a corresponding celestial orb.

Nyanonmilan: life-giving ceremony to a deity. Tamil Nadu.

Nila: indigo.

Nilgar: dyer.

Oddiyaanam: tight fitting stone-encrusted waist belt.

Odhni: head shawl.

Ona rakhna: floor paintings of Uttar Pradesh.

Ondoni: pot cushion.

Osa: floor paintings of Orissa.

Pallav: the decorated endpiece of saris and *dupattas* (shawls). Also, *muhun* or *anchal.*

Panchallar: silver- and goldsmiths.

Panchaloha: auspicious alloy of copper, tin, lead, silver and gold representing the five elements of earth, air, ether, water and fire, respectively.

Pandal: temporary cloth and bamboo temple for the festival of Dussehra.

Panni hari: design on a printed cotton cloth. Lit. 'the woman who brings water'.

Panniyaru: ledge or niche in the home where water is stored.

Pantoran: small embroidered, appliqué or patchwork frieze for the wall.

Paratha: unleavened bread.

Patila: large cooking vessels. Also, *karhai.*

Patola: double *ikat* silk cloth from Gujarat. Derived from the Sanskrit *pattakula*, 'silk cloth'.

Patri: pendant.

Pattu: silk.

Pavakathakali: puppet theatre; also name given to glove puppets of Kerala.

Perak: headdress of Ladakh.

Petigaras: wood-crafting community.

Phad: long rectangular narrative cloths.

Phukstel: large basket used for hauling fodder. Ladakh.

Phulkari: dowry embroidery of Punjab. Lit. 'flower work'.

Pichvai: painted cloth to hang behind the deity. Lit. 'something at the back'.

Pinjra: latticed wooden panel work. Kashmir.

Pintado: painted cloth, Portuguese.

Pipal: the leaf is used as a base for Indian miniature painting, especially in the south (*Ficus religiosa*).

Pongal: harvest festival of the south.

Pughri: turban.

Pujari: priest.

Purdah: veil.

Putul nauch: large dolls made of clay and rice husk modelled on a rod. West Bengal.

Raakkadi: circular hair decorations on the back of the head that depict a stone-encrusted swan.

Rabari: pastoral community of Gujarat and Rajasthan.

Raksha Bandhan: summer festival linking brothers and sisters.

Ramayana: Hindu epic.

Rangoli: floor paintings of Maharashtra.

Rangrez: dyer community. Lit. *rang,* 'colour', and *rez,* 'to pour'.

Raslila: theatre stories concerning the life of Krishna.

Ravanachhaya: shadow puppets of Orissa.

Rig Veda: sacred revelations of the Hindus.

Rotla: unleavened bread of millet flour.

Rudraksha: tree dedicated to Shiva (*Elaeocarpus ganitrus*).

Sadhu: ascetic.

Saffa: turban.

Sakhtasazi: process of papier mâché construction.

Sankia: L-shaped embroideries for the doorway.

Sari: unstitched women's garment.

Sarkanda: a type of grass.

Sathiya: floor paintings of Gujarat.

Sergars: silversmiths of Ladakh.

Shakstar: a floor matting of *chipkiang* reed. Ladakh.

Shali: fine rice.

Shankh: conch shell, symbol of good omen at temple, wedding ceremony and festival alike.

Shilpashastra: series of craft manuals of the early eleventh century.

Shisha: small mirrors as cloth decoration.

Shisham: grainy brown wood.

Shreni: guild.

Sikki: a type of grass.

Silavat: stone carving community.

Silpis: stonemasons.

Sits: Dutch for painted cloth.

Sompura: community of Gujarati stonemasons.

Sonar: silver- and goldsmith.

Sthapati: traditional architect-sculptor, master craftsman.

Sutradhar: woodworker. Lit. 'the holder of the line or rein'.

Tac'chan: wood carvers.

Tamil Mayamatha: treatise of the 10th century that guided the craftsmen of the Chola empire.

Taqri: girdle.

Tarkashi: gold, silver, copper or brass wire inlay in wood.

Tawa: round iron skillets for the cooking of unleavened bread.

Teh-nishan: an inlay of precious metal sheets in wood.

Thaali: marriage talisman. Also, *mangalasuthra.*

Thachar aahaari: carpenter, south India.

Thala: boss of a potter's wheel.

Thalaisaamaan: bejewelled head decoration.

Thap chabrik: large iron household stoves. Ladakh.

Thatera: workers in brass.

Thattan: jeweller.

Thavalai: cooking vessel for rice.

Ther: mobile platform for a temple deity.

Thewa: glass and gold ornamental work of Partabgarh, Rajasthan.

Tikka: spherical forehead pendant.

Tolpava koothu: shadow puppets of Kerala. Lit. *tol,* 'leather', *pava,* 'puppet' and *koothu,* 'story'.

Toran: embroidered, appliqué or patchwork frieze hung above the doorway.

Tsepo: basket for the carriage of vegetables to market. Ladakh.

Tulsi: sweet basil (*Ocimum sanctum*).

Tunglag: conch shell bangles. Ladakh.

Uruli: metal dish for cooking sweetmeats or vegetables.

Uthsavam: festival deity riding in a *ther.*

Vahana: processional mount for a deity.

Vaishnavite: follower of Vishnu.

Valai: a rack of bangles.

Vanki: inverted V-shaped decoration for the upper arm.

Varpu: very large platter-like metal cooking vessel.

Vira: supportive henchmen to Aiyanar.

Warlis: farming community of Maharashtra.

Yogi: wandering minstrel.

Zari: metal thread patterned cloth.

INDEX

SELECT BIBLIOGRAPHY

Anand, M. R., *Madhubani Painting*, 1984

Archana, *The Language of Symbols*, n.d.

Barnard, N., *Living with Decorative Textiles*, 1989

Birdwood, C. G. M., *The Industrial Arts of India*, 1880

Black, D., *The Unappreciated Dhurrie*, 1982

Chattopadhyay, K., *The Glory of Indian Handicrafts*, 1976

Chemould Publications and Arts, *The Warlis. Tribal Paintings and Legends*, n.d.

Collingwood, P., *Textile and Weaving Structures*, 1987

Coomaraswamy, A. K., *Arts and Crafts of India and Ceylon*, 1913

Coomaraswamy, A. K., *The Indian Craftsman*, 1909

Coomaraswamy, A. K., *Viswakarma: Examples of Indian Architecture, Sculpture, Painting, Handicraft*, 1914

Cooper, I., *The Guide to Painted Towns of Shekawati*, n.d.

Crafts Museum, New Delhi, *Mandana. A Folk Art of Rajasthan*, 1985

Dalmia, Y., *The Painted World of the Warlis*, 1988

Dhamija, J., *Indian Folk Arts and Crafts*, 1992

Elson, V. C., *Dowries from Kutch*, 1979

Emery, I., *The Primary Structure of Fabrics*, 1966

Folklore Museum, Udaipur, *Bhartiya Lok Kala Mandal*, 1988

Gillow, J. and Barnard, N., *Traditional Indian Textiles*, 1991

Hull, A. and Barnard, N., *Living with Kilims*, 1988

Huyler, S. P., *Village India*, 1985

Jain, J. and Aggarwala, A., *Museums of India: National Handicrafts and Handlooms Museum*, 1989

Jain, J., *Folk Art and Culture of Gujarat*, 1980

Jaitly, J. (ed.), *Crafts of Jammu, Kashmir & Ladakh*, 1990

Jaitly, J., *The Craft Traditions of India*, 1990

Jayakur, P., 'Traditional Textiles of India', *Marg.* XV, 4, 1962

Khanna, S., *Dynamic Folk Toys*, 1983

Kramrisch, S., *Unknown India: Ritual Art in Tribe & Village*, 1968

Krishna, N., *Arts and Crafts of Tamil Nadu*, 1992

Krishnankutty Pulavar, K. L., *Tolpava Koothu*, vol. 1, 1987

Mayer, A. C., *Caste and Kinship in Central India*, 1960

Mookerjee, A., *Folk Art of India*, 1986

Mookerjee, A., *Indian Dolls and Toys*, 1968

Mookerjee, A., *Ritual Art of India*, 1985

Nath, A. and Wacziarg, X. (eds), *Arts & Crafts of Rajasthan*, 1987

National Book Trust, *India. Festivals of India*, 1982

Nicholson, J., *The Traditional Arts of Gujarat*, 1988

Saraf, D. N., *Arts and Crafts of Jammu and Kashmir*, 1987

Saraf, D. N., *Indian Crafts*, 1982

Shah, H., *Form and Many Forms of Mother Clay*, 1985

Skelton, R., *Rajasthani Temple Hangings of the Krishna Cult*, 1973

Spear, P., *A History of India*, vol. 2, 1978

Thapar, R., *A History of India*, vol. 1, 1966

University of California, Los Angeles, *Asian Puppets: Wall of the World*, 1979

Venu, G., *Puppetry and Lesser Known Dance Traditions of India*, 1990

Welch, S. C., *India: Art and Culture 1300–1900*, 1988

ACKNOWLEDGMENTS

AUTHOR'S ACKNOWLEDGMENTS

In the planning and preparation for the journeys across India, I thank Richard and Marion Lightbown for their generous good advice and excellent contacts; Paul at Nomad of Turnpike Lane, London; Chris Thomas at Billingham Bags of Brierley Hill, West Midlands; Ravi at Arondale Travel, London; Daryl Timmins of East West Airlines of Bombay. Thanks are also due to Pat Wallace at Polaroid UK for supplying instant film; to Kiran Velagapudi for looking through proofs and for the loan of the *ikat* saris (p. 135); to Joss Graham who lent the *telia rumal* (p.135); to Bryan Sentence for generously providing masterful interpretations of obscure images; and to John Gillow, who was, as ever, a stalwart friend throughout the project and to whom I owe my appreciation of India.

Our travels were made the more agreeable by the generous hospitality of Goodie and Amrit Vohra and Shrivatsa Goswami and his family. Thanks are also due to Mr Tak, who proved the finest guide and a blissfully safe driver; Laxmi Narayan Shrimal, who was an excellent escort and friend; and Rajeev Kumar Jha and Bunty Bohra of Darbhanga for their introduction to the craftspeople of Mithila. One of our most memorable afternoons was spent in the company of the master puppeteer Krishnan Kutty Palavar and his sons in Kerala – we owe them much thanks for sharing their art. Finally, to those men and women of the state emporia who showed the way to many a craftsman, thank you.

This book is for my wife, who suffered our many partings whilst carrying the lovely Margaret.

Page 183: taken by the author

PHOTOGRAPHER'S ACKNOWLEDGMENTS

I would like to thank all those people who have helped to make the images in this book possible, especially Shrivatsa Goswami of Sri Caitanya Prem Samsthan, Vrindaban, Uttar Pradesh; Upendra Gupta of Clark's Hotel, Benares; Shamlu Dudeja in Calcutta; Raminak K. Shar in Bhuj, Gujarat; Bala Bharat of Televisual, Madras; Tsering Angdu of the Hotel Highland, Stok, Ladakh; Shail Choyal in Udaipur; S. Rajan from Thimmakudi, Tanjavore. Gracious credit is also due to the Handicrafts Museum at Pragati Maidan, New Delhi, and to FUJI Professional, in particular Graham Rutherford, for their continuing support.

Michael Duffy deserves special thanks for helping to create these images.